A YEAR AT
KEW

BBC
BOOKS

RUPERT SMITH

A YEAR AT KEW

CONTENTS

FOREWORD Alan Titchmarsh MBE VMH

I never thought of arguing with my boss in the Parks department nursery in Yorkshire. Well, I was only 15 and he seemed to have it all worked out. I would serve my apprenticeship while I worked for my City and Guilds examinations, and then I would spend a year studying full time at horticultural college, which would prepare me for three years at the Royal Botanic Gardens, Kew on the diploma course. Just like that. There was only one snag. Kew took about 20 students a year from the hundreds who applied.

For some unaccountable reason, the stern interviewers at Kew reckoned I was suitable student material, and in September 1969 I turned up for my first day's work. It was the start of a special relationship with a garden and it continues to this day.

But then, Kew is more than just a garden. It is both an historical tableau and the cutting edge of scientific research. Where once it ensured Britain's triumph in the colonies it now educates its gardeners, botanists and scientists, as well as the public, about the world's plants and how to conserve them for the future.

It is thirty-five years since I first set foot in the place, but it still holds a unique place in my affections. Whether I'm walking around the wilder parts of the arboretum gazing at the 'old lions' – the trees that are hundreds of years old – or marvelling at the giant waterlily in the Princess of Wales Conservatory, or remembering my year in the elegant Palm House, all my memories of Kew are happy ones.

Is this just the rose-tinted view of an old sentimentalist? Perhaps. But in the main it is the love of a gardener for the place that taught him his trade. Many of the plants I tended are still there. And so are many of the people I worked with. Who would work all their life in a place that did not hold some special kind of magic? 'Kewites' they call us. And I'm proud and happy to be one.

WELCOME TO KEW Professor Peter R. Crane frs, Director

All good gardens delight and inspire in different ways. On one hand their composition and arrangement is a work of art; on the other every plant embodies the power and beauty of nature. Each one tells a particular story about how life has evolved and is sustained on our planet. In these respects, as one of the world's great gardens, Kew is not unusual. But in other ways Kew is unique.

At Kew you can see stunning buildings reflecting three centuries of architectural style and innovation, you can experience a magnificent landscape that combines great beauty with outstanding historical significance, and you can explore the world's greatest collection of living plants. Kew is not just a garden, it is a phenomenon – a botanical powerhouse – unlike any other in the world.

As one of a select group of World Heritage Sites in the UK, Kew is recognized internationally as one of the world's most significant cultural landscapes. But it is also a globally important scientific organization, respected for the excellence of its work on the variety of plant life – its origins, its current status, and how it can be conserved and used in sustainable ways for human benefit. This research makes Kew a global leader in the science of plant diversity and a conservation organization that is making a real difference to the future of plants and people around the world.

But Kew is much more than just an organization with a long and distinguished history. It's also a vibrant community of remarkable people dedicated to under-standing plants and building a greater appreciation of the importance of conserving the world's plant resources. From leading horticulturists and scientists to those who work with the public or behind the scenes to ensure the smooth running of our programmes, Kew would not exist without these people, nor without continued support from the public, and the sponsorship of the Department for Environment, Food and Rural Affairs.

This book provides an intimate 'insider's view' of Kew. It follows Kew's magical beauty as the seasons change and introduces just a few of the very special people who work hard for Kew's visitors, for Kew's plants and for the broader international public who benefit from Kew and its work. All of us who work at Kew and Wakehurst Place, Kew's country estate, feel privileged to be part of a remarkable and globally-unique organization with an important mission. We hope you are similarly inspired by this insight into a year at Kew Gardens.

INTRODUCTION

Without royal connections, it's unlikely there would ever have been botanic gardens in the corner of southwest London now known as Kew. But as long ago as the fourteenth century English kings had established a presence in neighbouring Richmond – where a royal palace stood for 300 years until its destruction during the Commonwealth – and wherever royalty went, money was sure to follow. When the monarchy was restored in the latter half of the seventeenth century, Richmond and its adjoining areas once again became handy rural bolt holes for the aristocracy – and it's to this that we owe the growth of what is today Kew Gardens.

It was during the eighteenth century that the royal focus shifted from Richmond to Kew. In 1718 the Prince and Princess of Wales, later to become George II and Queen Caroline, moved to Richmond from London and started dividing up the estate. The Dutch House, built in 1631 and known today as Kew Palace, was one of the buildings on their land, in the nearby hamlet of Kew. In the 1730s their son and his wife, Prince Frederick and Princess Augusta, leased the estate of Kew, next to Richmond. Augusta was a keen gardener – and, after Frederick's death, it was she who started the botanic gardens on this site. She commissioned a collection that would, in the words of her friend and adviser the Earl of Bute, 'contain all the plants known on earth' – thus setting the standard for what would follow. When Augusta died in 1772 her son, George III, inherited the Kew estate, and in 1802 the Dutch House became his private home.

Like his mother, George was an enthusiastic gardener and after his accession to the throne in 1760 he had instructed Capability Brown to remodel a significant part of the Richmond estate in the new, natural style, removing several ornamental buildings in favour of broad, quasi-rural vistas and mixed plantings. By the time the Richmond and Kew estates were combined in 1802, the basic principles and design that can still be seen today at the Royal Botanic Gardens were in place.

For its royal residents, Kew was never just a collection of plants; the palace was a home, and the gardens were their private pleasure grounds. For his 17th birthday in 1755, the future George III had floated around the lake in a vast boat in the shape of a swan with outstretched wings, big enough to hold ten people.

OPPOSITE: Kew Palace, built in 1631, later became the private home of King George III.

In adult life he indulged his passion for agriculture by turning several acres over to turnips, barley and buckwheat, and grazing sheep on much of the rest (little wonder that he was nicknamed 'Farmer' George). Even George IV, who was widely accused of neglecting the estate, built impressive new gates and acquired a further 8 hectares (20 acres) for the estate.

The royal influence continued to shape Kew Gardens throughout the nineteenth and twentieth centuries. After a period of neglect and decline, the gardens were given to the public in 1840 at the start of Queen Victoria's reign – and so began a great expansion, with the building of monumental glasshouses and the upgrading of Kew to represent a centre of botanical excellence for the entire empire, a sort of outsize display case of imperial floral treasures. By the turn of the century, Kew had gained an international reputation as one of Europe's greatest collections of plants, and its place in history was secure.

THE LANDSCAPES

Kew presents to the visitor a bewildering array of different landscapes – from rural riverside fields to the formality of the Pagoda Vista, from the wildness of the woods to the tidiness of the decorative plantings. This is to a great extent the result of the piecemeal development of the gardens, with successive generations imposing their tastes on those of their forefathers; there was never a master plan for Kew, and it shows.

More than anything, the development of the gardens was shaped by two different, sometimes conflicting, factors. Firstly, there was the pure botanical desire to build up a collection, grouping trees and plants together by family or by country of origin, so that the whole of Kew became something like a living scientific library. Secondly, there was the landscaper's approach, which was concerned with creating beauty at the expense of science. Kew's first full-time director, William Hooker (appointed in 1840), was constantly arguing with his landscape designer, William Nesfield, about the purpose of their charge – Nesfield complaining, frequently and bitterly, that Hooker's obsession with taxonomy and planned plantings was stifling his creativity. Hooker, for his part, despised

Nesfield's pandering to visitors, and in 1865 handed the directorship of the gardens over to his son Joseph, who believed that the whole enterprise would have made more headway without 'pleasure seekers', as he called them.

Between these two extremes Kew developed into what its historian, Ray Desmond, described as 'a palimpsest of garden styles', where different tastes and different phases overlay each other, where history is written in the shape of a flower bed, the slope of a lawn, the planting of a coppice.

Against all odds — and this, perhaps, is the essence of Kew's magic — all these conflicting forces have combined to create a harmonious whole. William Nesfield, despite his fights with William Hooker, created a framework of vistas and avenues that remains the backbone of modern Kew Gardens. The Broad Walk, the pond at the front of the Palm House and the vistas that radiate from behind are all his work, and it's been the concern of more recent custodians to return Nesfield's creations to their original glory. The Broad Walk has been replanted with cedars, and a ten-year replanting programme for the Pagoda Vista was put in place in 2004 — part of a commitment to keep alive a unique heritage of garden design.

ABOVE: The decorative features of the Queen's Garden, which lies behind Kew Palace, reflect seventeeth-century fashions.

THE ARBORETUM

More than anything else, Kew is a great collection of trees – an 'arboretum'. They've been brought here from all over the world since Capability Brown first planted up what was then part of George III's Richmond estate in the 1760s, and every time the boundaries of the gardens have expanded more trees have been brought in to fill the space. But it was under William Hooker that the arboretum really began to take shape. With his love of order, he carved the gardens up so that different spaces would provide a home for different genera of trees; by 1849 Kew as a whole contained more than 2000 species.

The arboretum today takes up about two-thirds of the overall area of Kew Gardens, and contains something in the region of 14,000 trees. Hooker's framework can still be seen in the sudden changes of species – but, gradually, there's a move towards planting schemes that reflect naturally occurring habitats. The overall collection divides into seven main regions, each with its own character, its own seasonal highlights and its own unique history.

The Woodland Glade, to the west of the Temperate House, contains Kew's real giants – the Californian redwoods and other huge conifers, underplanted with shrubs to break up the gloom. It's a quiet, mysterious place, particularly around the Waterlily Pond, which it encloses.

The Berberis Dell started life as a gravel pit just north of the Flagpole; in 1869 work began to empty this and make a sunken garden which was planted up with a colourful flowering collection, including mahonias and a wide variety of berberis. Like the Rhododendron Dell, it's one of Kew's more surprising features – hard to see from a distance, but once you dip down into it, particularly at the height of the flowering season in early summer, or when the autumn fruits are in full colour, it's a dazzling sight.

Much of the arboretum is planted for visual effect – the maples that run between the Temperate House and the Flagpole are dazzling in autumn, while Cherry Walk, which runs from the Rose Garden behind the Palm House along to the Temperate House, boasts a spectacular collection of Japanese ornamental cherries, replanted in 1996. Holly Walk, laid out by Joseph Hooker in 1874, marks the course of the old Love Lane from Kew to Richmond and retains many of the original trees – an amazing sight in December, when the berries are at their brightest. Moisture-loving trees are grouped round the lake, blending into the Pinetum and Conifer Trail, one of the biggest collections of trees in the gardens.

THE GLASSHOUSES

Kew's glasshouses are its most famous features – they're the focus of many people's visits, home to some spectacular plant specimens and architectural marvels in their own right. The Palm House is the oldest and remains, at least in design terms, the most impressive – the one truly unmistakable icon of Kew Gardens. It was built between 1844 and 1848 to designs by Decimus Burton, who strove for an elegant simplicity of form – a radical departure from the then-prevalent taste for all things ornate, arched and Gothic. Burton's designs were realized by Richard Turner, an engineer whose understanding of shipbuilding technology made it possible for the enormous open span of the Palm House to stand without too much internal support.

The Palm House was always envisaged as a focal point. It's deliberately reflected in the pond on its east side, while the Pagoda Vista and Syon Vista both radiate from its axis. And, in true Victorian style, function was never allowed to detract from form: the pipework and chimneys that withdrew the smoke from the underground boilers that heated the glasshouse were buried, running for 149 metres (490 feet) to emerge in the great ornate Campanile – in essence a giant chimney.

The Palm House is a delicate structure and has frequently been restored. In 1955, after a century of heat and steam, it was in a bad way. The coal-fired boilers, which had never done a particularly good job and were prone to flooding, were moved out of the basement and new, oil-fired boilers were installed behind the Campanile. The building was completely reglazed and the metalwork was realigned. This kept it going for a while, but by the 1980s it was apparent that the whole structure needed a radical makeover. Between 1984 and 1988 the Palm House was emptied for the first time ever. Although most of the palms were kept in temporary storage, some were too big to move and had to be cut down. The shell was then dismantled and rebuilt, piece by piece, using toughened safety glass and modern, lightweight glazing bars. The replanted Palm House was reopened by the Queen Mother in 1990.

Bigger, but easier to manage, is the Temperate House – Kew's biggest public glasshouse and the world's largest surviving Victorian glass structure. Another Decimus Burton design, covering 4880 square metres (52,500 square feet) – twice the size of the Palm House – it didn't get off to a good start. Burton's original budget of £10,000 was wildly exceeded when the contractor put in a bill for nearly three times that amount. The Treasury called a halt to the work, begun in 1860, when only the centre section and the octagons were complete. The project wasn't resumed until 1895 – the south wing was built, but then the contractor went bankrupt, forcing another delay. The second wing wasn't completed until 1899.

Alongside Kew's iconic Victorian glasshouses, which also include the Waterlily House, built in 1852, stand two modern neighbours – the Princess of Wales Conservatory (opened in 1987 to commemorate Princess Augusta, founder of the gardens) and the Evolution House.

SPECIAL GARDENS AND BUILDINGS

People who know Kew well are familiar with the many smaller, 'secret' gardens that nestle among its more famous features. The Duke's Garden, for instance, is a rare example of a planting in Kew designed almost entirely for pleasure, rather than for science or utility. Attached to the former home of the Duke of Cambridge (known as 'Cambridge Cottage') it was incorporated into the public gardens on the duke's death in 1904, complete with a fine collection of herbaceous perennials around large lawns. The Queen's Garden, attached to Kew Palace, is another marvel of formal planting, with clipped box hedges surrounding immaculate parterres, an ornamental pond and a selection of statues. It looks like the perfect seventeenth-century garden – but don't be fooled. The Queen's Garden is strictly 'repro': it was designed by Sir George Taylor, then director of the Royal Botanic Gardens, in 1959. Taylor was a stickler for authenticity, and all the plants in the garden were found in Britain before and during the seventeenth century.

Not all Kew's special gardens are so formal. The Woodland Garden, just northeast of the Palm House pond, replicates nature's designs with a deciduous canopy, a layer of shrubs and a selection of ground-cover plants including hellebores, primulas, poppies and trilliums. The Grass Garden, designed in 1982, gives prominence to plants that are often taken for granted but which, planted in the right way, form one of the highlights of Kew in winter. And for those with a sweet tooth, the Bee Garden contains not only the flowers favoured by bees – it also contains hives where the sought-after Kew honey is produced. Other gardens are given over to lilacs, roses, rhododendrons, azaleas, magnolias, bamboos and alpines, ensuring that there's something for visitors to see at any time of the year.

In addition to the gardens, there's Kew's quirky collection of buildings. Some of these are functional: the Marianne North Gallery, for instance, houses a collection of work by the great Victorian botanical artist. Some, like the Japanese Gateway, are integral parts of specific plantings. But there are many that are gloriously pointless, remnants of a fashion for purely decorative architecture that

has long since passed. The Ruined Arch, the temples of Bellona, Arethusa and Aeolus, King William's Temple… none of these serves any function, but each one complements the landscape in a special way. The most famous, and most visible, of the ornamental buildings is the Pagoda – completed in 1762, and a lasting monument to the eighteenth-century taste for all things elaborate and Chinese. The ten-storey structure stands nearly 50 metres (165 feet) high, and survived German bombs during the Second World War.

EDUCATION AND RESEARCH

Behind the scenes there is a huge range of activities that goes largely unseen by the public. The Kew School of Horticulture is recognized as one of the great centres of excellence in the gardening world; graduates of its diploma course include some of the best-known names in horticulture today. However, education at Kew isn't limited to the school; the gardens are run specifically to educate visitors about the world in which they live, and to provide expert advice and information to students of botany and horticulture from all over the world. The Herbarium houses an extraordinary collection of plant samples from the eighteenth century onwards – including some that were collected by Charles Darwin himself.

As well as disseminating information, Kew also collects it. In the Jodrell Laboratory a team of scientists works on a wide range of projects, from cutting-edge medical research to authentication work for commercial clients. For these scientists, the plant world is a vast, untapped resource that could yield astonishing results – anything from new, bug-resistant crop strains for Third World farmers to a cure for cancer.

WAKEHURST PLACE

There's more to the Royal Botanic Gardens than the world-famous Kew site; there is also Kew's 'country cousin', at Wakehurst Place in the heart of the High Sussex Weald. This estate was leased from the National Trust in 1965, and since then it has become an increasingly important complement to the London site. The magnificent mansion on which the gardens centre dates from the Elizabethan period, but it wasn't until the early twentieth century that the property became associated with horticulture. Over a period of more than 30 years, from 1903, Gerald Loder, the first Lord Wakehurst, built up an extraordinary collection of plants from all over the world – and by the time Wakehurst Place was given to the nation in 1963 it boasted a huge mature garden of international importance.

Wakehurst Place isn't just a pretty garden. The Royal Botanic Gardens' conservation mission is amply demonstrated by the Loder Valley Nature Reserve, a site of Special Scientific Interest that combines woodland, meadowland and

ABOVE: The open vistas at Kew are one of the reasons for its popularity. Benches are placed around the Lake so that visitors and staff alike can enjoy the views towards Syon House, on the other side of the River Thames.

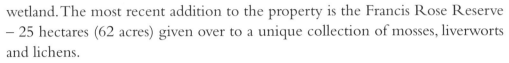

wetland. The most recent addition to the property is the Francis Rose Reserve – 25 hectares (62 acres) given over to a unique collection of mosses, liverworts and lichens.

But the star attraction at Wakehurst Place, at least in terms of media interest, is the Millennium Seed Bank – an extraordinary new building that already houses the seeds of 95 per cent of British flora, and will soon preserve 10 per cent of the world's. In total, that's something like 24,000 plant species that will be housed, preserved and protected for hundreds of years at Wakehurst Place.

KEW AS A WORLD HERITAGE SITE

On 3 July 2003, a UNESCO meeting in Paris announced that the Royal Botanic Gardens, Kew had officially been inscribed on the list of World Heritage Sites. It's a major pat on the back for an organization that's been quietly contributing to a global understanding of gardening, conservation and science since 1759, and for the Kew staff who have dedicated so much time and energy to their work it's an important encouragement. 'It's a superb international endorsement of the importance of Kew,' says director Peter Crane. 'In recent years there's been a trend away from naming western European places as World Heritage Sites, and there have been plenty of other applications that have come away from Paris unsuccessfully. So this is a major feather in our cap. It's good to be among the best of the best.'

Regular visitors to the gardens can be in no doubt that Kew is one of the most beautiful, magical places in the world – but it is its other, special, qualities that make it worthy of such major status. On a garden design level it is important because of its landscape, sculpted by leading garden designers, including Capability Brown, and its buildings by William Chambers; and in historical terms, it played a key role in the discovery of plants and the spread of knowledge about the plant kingdom. Today, Kew is world-renowned as a centre of scientific expertise.

'I was never in any doubt that we had a good case,' says Crane, 'but I made sure our application was as strong as it could be.' To this end, he and his team scoured the history books for examples of the garden's contribution to an appreciation of plants. It was clear that Kew was designed to look as natural as possible from the start – this at a time when the fashion was for artificial gardens – and that this naturalness has always been its most distinctive quality. It was in the vanguard of environmental gardening in the late eighteenth century, and it still is, with its emphasis on conservation and education. Along the way, the team discovered fascinating titbits from the garden's history – for example, why the Temperate House is where it is, so far from a gate. The reason? The original plans for Kew Gardens underground station placed it at the end of an avenue that would have led straight to the Temperate House. However, by the time the glasshouse was built, plans had changed and the station was moved elsewhere.

UNESCO's endorsement of Kew is important in raising the Royal Botanic Gardens' international profile, and in keeping visitor numbers high. Big commercial sponsors are also likely to be attracted by Kew's new status, and without this kind of business partnership it would be impossible for Kew to continue its programme of work. This recognition of what Kew is doing is a major vindication of its basic principles. In recent years the aim has been to focus activities on specific goals, and this was emphasized in the application. In terms of visitors, for instance, the main objective is education – specifically about conservation, so that people leave the gardens with a clear message about the diversity of plants in the world, and the threats to that diversity. On the scientific side, every project has been re-examined to make sure it is worth doing. Kew has always worked to the highest scientific standards, but now it is a question of whether what it is doing will make a difference in the world. 'It's not enough to take a back seat in the area of biodiversity,' says Crane. 'If we're interested in the natural world, we have to focus on protecting it.'

JANUARY

The trees are bare, and on a clear January day you can see from one end of the garden to the other. It's the quietest time of year in terms of visitor numbers – but Kew is never idle. In the arboretum and the glasshouses it's a time for pruning and cleaning, undisturbed by spring and summer crowds. And while the plants may be largely dormant, the wildlife is anything but. Look up into the trees for glimpses of goldcrests and siskins, or flocks of common species like chaffinches, tits and blackbirds, making the most of abundant food resources on the short winter days. The tamer birds – robins, or even pheasants – might even feed out of your hand.

This month at Kew, don't miss

- Snowdrops throughout the gardens
- Witch hazels by King William's Temple
- Hellebores in the Order Beds and viburnums round the Palm House pond
- The Duchess Border outside the Duke's Garden
- Dogwoods and witch hazels in the specimen beds, Wakehurst Place

OPPOSITE: *Winter at Kew is a special time of year. The gardens look magical after a heavy snowfall and the lake often freezes around the edges.*

TREE PLANTING

With the ground at Kew wetter and softer than it is throughout the summer and autumn, January is the best time for planting broadleaf trees. And in January 2004, six 10-metre (33-foot) trees were added to the Pagoda Vista to fill gaps in the avenue, the result of storms and disease in recent years. It was the start of a ten-year programme that aims to return the vista to its original magnificence, and it was important to incorporate fully grown specimens that would fit into the overall design like missing pieces in a jigsaw.

These days the choice of trees brought into Kew is guided by the changing English climate, so Tony Kirkham, head of the arboretum, and his team look to the eastern seaboard of the United States and to Asia Minor for ones that can withstand long, hot summers and cold winters. Three different varieties make up the half a dozen specimens bought for the Pagoda Vista: Turkish hazel and two American species, sweet gum and pin oak. Specially selected for their longevity at Kew, these are well suited to the weather here and also make good avenue trees, with stately trunks and broad, near-symmetrical crowns. They provide year-round interest, and are particularly good autumn performers. Unlike home-grown trees, which are planted out when they are young, these specimens were chosen on the basis of their mature shape; it's a rare example of aesthetic considerations overriding other botanical factors.

Planting a semi-mature tree isn't a simple matter of digging a hole and dropping a tree into it, in a roughly upright position. Some months before planting starts the ground is broken up with rotavators and tractor-mounted spading machines, in order to allow the late autumn rainfall to penetrate the ground, making digging easier and providing enough moisture to sustain the tree without irrigation. Then a hole big enough to accommodate a root ball about 1.5 metres (5 feet) in diameter, with room to grow, is dug. After this the hard part starts. Cranes are brought in to lift the tree into an upright position and lower it into the hole. Once this has been done the root ball is stabilized to minimize movement – without some kind of fixing system the tree could blow around in a high wind, damaging new roots. A network of cables is thrown over the top of the root ball and secured in the ground, applying a downward pressure to the base of the plant

that limits movement. This is buried when the hole is backfilled, and the tree can then settle down. The process takes about two hours, from digging the hole to completing the backfilling – and it's very popular with visitors.

January is also the time when Kirkham and his team set out the new young trees that have been grown in Kew's in-house nurseries from seed brought back from foreign expeditions. This is when Kirkham sees the fruits of his globe-trotting – particularly his Chinese expeditions. The trees, about two years old and less than a metre in height, can be seen throughout the collections in the arboretum – part of Kew's extraordinary annual investment in biodiversity.

ABOVE: Kew's arboretum is replenished whenever necessary. Six semi-mature trees were planted in Pagoda Vista in 2004, to fill a gap near the Palm House where trees had died.

THE STORY OF A SEED

All the Millennium Seed Bank's collection is sourced from the wild – but this doesn't mean that *any* wild seed will make it into the Seed Bank. Some material just isn't suitable for long-term storage, while other seeds don't meet standards set by a rigorous process developed by the Seed Conservation Department.

The first test comes in the field when seeds are sourced from wild plants. Anything that's going to be stored for a long time has to be able to survive in dry conditions – it has to be 'dessication tolerant' – and although most seeds are able to dry, it certainly isn't the case for all species. The seeds of long-lived woody perennials, such as oaks, for instance, are often not able to withstand dryness, so it's impossible to keep their seeds in the Millennium Seed Bank. These plants tend to be dominant in their habitats, and therefore there's less need for the seeds to last – nature has other ways of ensuring the success of these species, allowing them to compete successfully with other plants. Dessication tolerance is decided on in the field; there's no point packing up and shipping seeds that won't be of any use at Wakehurst Place.

The seeds of almost 90 per cent of the remaining plants can be successfully banked, provided they're at the right stage. Harvesting them too early, before they are ripe, greatly undermines their chances of long-term survival. When to harvest needs to be judged by an expert eye – there are telltale signs depending on the species, like the colour of the fruit or the seed's coat, and the hardness of the seed (which can be tested with the teeth). Seeds get tougher and harder as they lose moisture, and some won't store successfully if they're too wet and soft.

Drying seed for transportation is a delicate business. It's not a good idea to do this too soon after collection; a long, slow dessication is better as it more closely resembles what would happen to the plant in its natural habitat. Some seed matter dries on the plant, but much of it remains connected to the parent plant at the time of collection and has to have a period of ambient drying before any further treatment. It's the same process as cutting a foxglove head and leaving it to dry on newspaper in a potting shed. The right drying conditions at this stage can have a huge influence on the seeds' long-term survival.

Once the seed has dried under ambient conditions, it's packaged and shipped to Wakehurst Place where the really intensive work begins. The seeds are taken out of their packaging and put uncleaned into the Seed Bank's dry room, in conditions of 18 per cent relative humidity and about 20°C (68°F). This dries the seed out so that it has an even lower moisture content and reduces the chance of loss dramatically. It's not a difficult atmosphere to maintain, so this stage of the seeds' processing is not expensive in terms of air conditioning or refrigeration. The seeds aren't kept in darkness; some of them need further light in order to mature, particularly those in green pods.

With loose seeds, sight and touch are enough to tell how they are maturing. Harder to gauge are ones hidden inside large, fleshy fruits like squash. These come to Wakehurst Place as complete fruits, and finding out whether or not a longer period in the dry room will improve their longevity is a process of trial and error.

BELOW: Three giant seed sculptures by Randal Page stand outside the entrance to the Millennium Seed Bank at Wakehurst Place.

When the seeds are ready, all the cleaning is done by hand. It takes a long time – and if commercial seed-producers used equally slow methods they'd soon go out of business – but it's the only way to ensure that the seeds get the best possible attention. It is important at this stage to avoid any action that might shorten their lifespan. Vigorous sieving of delicate grass seeds, for instance, is a very effective way of producing flour – but is not so great for producing bankable seed.

After fruiting material and other non-essentials have been cleaned away, the seeds are screened to see whether they are fertile. Gentle winnowing within an enclosed environment blows away the lighter, infertile ones, while X-rays reveal the tiny plant embryos waiting to germinate. In a natural or commercial setting, it's not important to weed out all the infertile seeds; in the Seed Bank, however, all the seed must be 'good', if the next step of the process is to make any sense.

After cleaning and screening, fertile seeds are dried for a further month sealed in containers, then banked at temperatures of -20°C (-4°F). Finally, within six months, seeds face the final hurdle – the germination test – when samples are taken out to be germinated. It's the only way to be certain that the seeds in the bank will survive: if they have been through every stage of the process, including cold storage, they are likely to survive for a long time.

Seeds are germinated in agar jelly in a Petri dish and, depending on the plant type, are subjected to variations in light and temperature that should encourage growth. Some seeds need light that's very rich in the red end of the spectrum, to replicate the light waves in direct sunlight. Some benefit from temperature fluctuations, to replicate the pattern of day and night. Seeds from the pea family appreciate a bit of rough handling; they have watertight skins, which have to be chipped in order to let in moisture and trigger germination – in the wild this would be done by rough weather or by passing through the digestive tract of an animal. In nature, some seeds need a cold winter in order to germinate in the spring, while others need a period of wet weather. Knowing the habits of different plant groups means botanists can create the ideal conditions for each seed.

Germination is considered to have been successful when the emerging root tips become 'geotropic' – in other words, start pointing downwards, trying to bury themselves in the earth. At this point, any unwanted germinated seeds are incinerated. The Seed Bank is governed by strict rules, which prevent any of its material being used in inappropriate ways by third parties.

Eighty per cent of all seed collections germinate successfully at the hands of the curation team. The remaining difficult 20 per cent are handed over to the Seed Bank's technologists for further experiments, and they manage to bring on a further 80 per cent of this 20 per cent. Any seed collections that have still not germinated, are passed on to researchers at Wakehurst Place who take a long-term look at particular seed types and assess their suitability for banking.

TREE OF THE MONTH
Chestnut-leaved oak *Quercus castaneifolia*

LOCATION: Lawn behind the Waterlily House

DID YOU KNOW: This mighty oak is one of Kew's great survivors – during the hurricane in 1987 it didn't budge an inch. In fact, as other oaks tumbled all across the gardens, the chestnut leaved oak didn't lose a single limb. Now it's one of the biggest broadleaf trees in Kew, at over 30 metres (nearly 100 feet) tall and 30 metres (nearly 100 feet) wide.

The species comes from the Caucasus and Iran, and was originally introduced to Britain in the form of seed, proving once again that great oaks really do from little acorns grow. This particular tree – which has been designated as a champion tree by the Tree Register of the British Isles (TROBI), and is the largest of its kind anywhere in Britain – was planted in 1846, and continues to grow.

HARVESTING SEED

ROGER SMITH
Leader of Millennium
Seed Bank Project

Kew has always had a seed bank of sorts – back in the old days it was just a large version of what every gardener does at the end of the season, collecting and drying seed from plants and then sharing it with friends. The Seed Conservation Department had already conserved about 1.5 per cent of the world's flora.

All that changed when the Millennium Commission set us the challenge of increasing our seed bank to hold all the native British flora and a further 10 per cent of the world's flora by 2010. They gave us a big budget for the project, and provided the money to create the new building at Wakehurst Place. The Millennium Seed Bank is now up and running, and we've already collected 95 per cent of the UK flora – that's nearly 1400 species. The things we haven't yet managed to get are plants that are recorded as seeding in the UK but we don't know how often, so there may come a point where we have to cross certain things off the list if we really don't think they're seeding in this country any more.

The larger task is the collection of the further 24,200 species that make up that target of 10 per cent of the world's flora. We've calculated that, in order to meet the deadline, we've got to look at eight different species for every working day of the project up till 2010 – and they all have to go through the entire process of cleaning and testing, and ultimately into storage. Many of the species will have seeds that science hasn't really looked at closely before, so there's a great deal of information to process as well as the actual seed material. Every new plant that we're dealing with adds to a body of information about seed collection and preservation techniques, and we're hoping to feed that information back to the countries of origin, so this really is a two-way process. It would be pointless if all the material just came here and that was the end of it; where would the benefit be for the partner countries if that was the case?

We're working mostly with dryland countries, and in the last year we've had expeditions to the USA, Mexico,

Chile, South Africa, Namibia, Kenya, Mali, Malawi, Burkina Faso, Syria, Lebanon, Australia and a few other countries. One of the most interesting and important areas we work in is Madagascar, because there are so many unique species of both animals and plants there that we have to work hard to preserve ones that are disappearing fast. If something is endangered in Madagascar, you can be certain that it's endangered worldwide, because so many of those plants just don't occur anywhere else. Our partner in Madagascar is a forester, and this is an important opportunity for us to learn something about the vigorous business of Third World forestry, and for them to learn something about the conservation concerns of botanists. It's a very important cross-cultural exchange.

Our collecting programmes are guided by a set of principles that I can sum up most simply as the three Es: Endangered, Endemic and Economic. Obviously if a plant is disappearing in the wild, there's a sense of urgency about collecting and preserving the seed. If it's endemic to a certain area, we need to record that information and look at possible future programmes of reintroduction. And we have a particular interest in plants that are of economic use to the rural poor — that's where the real interface between plants and people takes place. There are 6300 species listed as being of importance to the rural poor in the Survey of Economic Plants of the Arid and Semi-Arid Lands — and they can be anything from wild plants that are used for food, like varieties of pea, millet, rice and sorghum, through to certain types of euphorbia that are used as living fences to pen cattle, or a particular thorn bush that gives good twigs that can be used as toothbrushes. It's a grey area between wild plants and agriculture.

If a plant has local value and is also becoming scarce, then it's particularly important to us. You never know what's likely to happen in the country of origin. A plant might start dying out, and so people might realize its value and seek to protect it. On the other hand, they might see it disappearing and just harvest the whole lot there and then. In either case, the role of the Seed Bank is important. Obviously if we don't see the preferred outcome, we've collected a stock of seed that could be used for reintroduction in the future. But even if the plant is protected, it's a good idea to take the seed material to labs in Europe and North

America, where there are better research facilities, because there's much more likelihood of useful discoveries being made there, which can be sent back to the country of origin and used to improve the sustainability of that resource. It's a bit like Kew's old role in the days of the British Empire when it was, to a great degree, a school for plantation management. Now I think we have a much less paternalistic, intrusive role to play — we're able to disseminate our knowledge about plants in a way that will benefit the people who need them.

PLANT OF THE MONTH

Witch hazel *Hamamelis*

WHERE TO SEE IT: Around King William's Temple; throughout the gardens at Kew and Wakehurst Place

DID YOU KNOW: The witch hazel is one of the outstanding performers of the winter months, adding colour and scent to the gardens at a time when not much else is out. The spidery, yellow or orange flowers appear on bare twigs well before the leaves — which have their own burst of glory in the autumn.

Witch hazels have raised concerns about climate change in the south of England. They're starting to flower earlier and earlier at Wakehurst Place — as early as August in some cases. The odd summer flower isn't unusual there, but the mass blooming in recent years means the plants haven't been at their best in winter, when they're most needed. Strangely, the same thing isn't happening at Kew, where the witch hazels continue to put on their major show in the dark weeks of January.

At its crudest level, the Seed Bank is an insurance policy against things dying out in the wild. There was a lot of excitement about the project when it first launched, and people really wanted to see us as an instant cure for all the world's ills. But we're part of a much wider process. When world leaders signed up to the Convention on Biological Diversity at the Rio Earth Summit in 1992, they were acting on the wishes of the people who elected them – and we're doing our bit to deliver some of the objectives of the convention. But it's not our job to deliver all those objectives; that would be well beyond Kew's core business. We do what we can, then we pass the baton on to our partners. The Seed Bank is a source of research and a source of materials, and we're establishing links with people in our source countries who will take what we can give and use it. Any seed that comes from us will be easily germinable if you need to use it for reintroduction, and it will be of a high standard for research purposes. But it's not down to Kew to preserve the world's flora all alone. This is just a link in the chain.

We have to be careful about what happens to material from the Seed Bank; we can't just give it out willy-nilly. We have a consent agreement with all the countries we collect from that we will control the material, and there are many reasons for this. For one thing, we have to protect ourselves against invasive foreign plant species, and against diseases. But there's a wider economic picture as well. If we were giving material out to commercial enterprises there's a chance there could be a considerable financial benefit, and that should really go back to the country of origin as much as possible. I think people overestimate the potential of 'green gold' in natural species; if there really was a huge amount of money to be made from natural collection, people would be raking it in left, right and centre. But say, for instance, you could find a gene in a certain dryland species that gives the plant drought-resistance; plant scientists would be very interested in getting hold of that and jockeying those genes along inside wheat. If that's the case, the country of origin should get a cut of the money.

We'll supply seed to any bona fide research institute or commercial company on the understanding that we'll share any created wealth with our partners. It's a controversial area at the moment because as soon as anyone mentions genetic engineering we get drowned in political rhetoric from people who don't have a complete understanding of the subject. Kew isn't in a position to educate government officials in the the commercial realities of economic crops; I don't think the Chancellor of the Exchequer is going to wake up any day now thinking, 'Damn! I wish I'd gone to the Millennium Seed Bank at Kew before I made that decision!'. But it's an area in which countries are going to have to learn quickly.

My approach to the work of the Seed Bank is pretty simple. I always think that if we can do something to protect plant species, then we should. There's no point in saying, 'Well, we could have done that, but for whatever reason, we didn't, and now it's too late.' When I'm in my dotage, being wheeled up and down Hove seafront in a bath chair, and I'm tackled by gangs of cheeky boys who say, 'What did you do for plant conservation?', I want to be able to say we used simple, inexpensive methods to preserve seeds, and that the plant has continued in the wild as well, which is the win–win outcome. What I don't want to say is that we took a gamble and didn't preserve seed materials, then things went the wrong way and we've lost the species. Surprisingly, it was Mrs Thatcher who said that no generation owns the world freehold; we just have it on a full repairing lease. When the time comes for my generation to hand the world on, I want it to be in the best possible repair.

What we're doing here at Wakehurst is very much what we all do in our gardens, or in our village horticultural societies. We're learning through trial and error, and we're growing in confidence as we work with partners, and as time goes by there's a little bit of friendly rivalry between us. It's the same competition that you might have with your neighbour, or that you might see at the Chelsea Flower Show. We have a certain amount of rivalry with our partners around the world, on the understanding that we're working towards a common interest of preserving plants.

FEBRUARY

The worst of the winter is past and the hours of daylight are gradually increasing. The gardens respond by bursting into bloom. Snowdrops give way to daffodils and crocuses, flowering as far as the eye can see. The garden birds start to pair off in preparation for the mating season, and around the lakes and ponds, frogs and toads are spawning in vast numbers. Along the Riverside Walk you'll see cormorants flying to and from their nesting grounds in ever-increasing flocks. Everywhere you look the gardens and their inhabitants are gearing up for the full frenzy of spring.

This month at Kew, don't miss

- Snowdrops throughout the gardens
- Rhododendrons starting to flower in the Rhododendron Dell
- The beautiful blooms of *Clematis cirrhosa*
- Spring bulbs at Wakehurst Place in the entrance area and the Slips
- Kew's annual Orchid Festival
- 1.6 million crocuses below the Temple of Bellona between Victoria Gate and King William's Temple towards the end of the month
- Daffodils along the Broad Walk in late February

OPPOSITE: *During the winter, Kew's magnificent Victorian Palm House is often beautifully lit by the low afternoon sun.*

CARNIVOROUS PLANTS

ABOVE: *The Venus flytrap is just one of Kew's growing collection of carnivorous plants, which are housed in the Princess of Wales Conservatory once they are ready to leave the nurseries.*

Spring starts a little early in Kew's nurseries, where advanced techniques of propagation allow the team to achieve spectacular results raising some of the world's most difficult, delicate plants. Micropropagation techniques can ensure the germination of the tiniest, most sensitive seeds – among them orchids and carnivorous plants like pitcher plants – where more traditional methods are hit-and-miss. Seeds are raised in a sterile environment, placed on a bed of agar and fed a cocktail of hormones and fertilizers that ensures healthy cell division. It's an amazingly successful method of propagating plants, with a near 100 per cent success rate.

February is the time when the tiny plantlets that have been raised by micropropagation have to leave their sterile jars and make a start in the real world. Once they are about the size of lettuce seedlings that are ready to be planted out they're carefully divided and introduced into non-sterile soil. It's important to get the plants out early enough for them to develop proper root systems; if they are kept in agar and soaked with the hormone and fertilizer mixture for too long they will not survive on their own. The new plants are planted up into a special soil mix and placed in a propagator tank where the roots form – after which they are ready to be added to collections throughout the gardens. This is a good method for raising orchids, and there's a high demand for these stunning flowers at the time of Kew's annual orchid festival.

Micropropagation has also been the key to maintaining Kew's collection of carnivorous plants, which produce tiny seeds that are very hard to raise in more conventional circumstances. Carnivores like pitcher plants, sundews and Venus flytraps are strange beings. They've developed a taste for insects because they grow in boggy conditions where there are next to no nutrients in the substrate, and they

February

Snowdrop *Galanthus nivalis*

WHERE TO SEE THEM: Rock Garden in Kew;
  woodland throughout Kew and Wakehurst Place

DID YOU KNOW: Snowdrops come in a variety of
  shapes and sizes, but the small white flowers we all
  know and love as early harbingers of spring are at
  their best when naturalized. They do well throughout
  Kew's arboretum, but are also well established in the
  Natural Areas, where they can spread unchecked.
  Many of the most flourishing patches of snowdrops
  in Kew are the result of almost haphazard plantings –
  bulbs were placed around the bases of trees in years
  gone by.

need to find supplements. This works well in nature, but in a nursery it's hard to replicate the conditions that will lead to germination. Micropropagation, however, can provide the seeds with exactly the right nutrients – or lack thereof – to ensure a new batch of plants for each yield of seed.

The carnivorous collection is not only growing in size – it's also growing in popularity. Children, especially, love these freaks of the plant world, and particularly enjoy the larger pitcher plants which throw out traps big enough to take a rat. But the specimens at Kew don't bite. Instead of catching insects, which don't come into the glasshouses in great numbers, they rely on liquid feed, which is strictly rationed to ensure that the plants produce plenty of their trademark traps. Too well fed, and the carnivores will grow large leaves and no traps; underfed, they'll exhaust themselves. With Kew's carnivorous collection, it's a definite case of 'treat 'em mean to keep 'em keen'.

FESTIVAL OF ORCHIDS

Part of Kew's orchid collection is permanently on display in the Princess of Wales Conservatory, but this is just the tip of the iceberg. There isn't room to show the 5000-plus plants that form the entire holding – and so, every February, Kew gives itself over to an orchid orgy, celebrating the exoticism and variety of this most collectable of plants. It's one of the first big highlights of the calendar year, bringing an explosion of colour to the gardens at a time when visitors and staff alike are happy to step out of the cold, grey, end of winter and into something altogether more uplifting.

Planning the species displays for the orchid festival is a year-round job that's overseen by Phil Griffiths, manager of the glasshouses, and Steve Ruddy from Information Services Support. At the end of every festival they look at what's done well, which species have thrived, and which designs have worked best to bring the collection to life. During the spring and summer they'll bring on the plants that will form the heart of the following February's display; most of the orchid collection is housed in the nursery and is not open to the public on a daily basis. Here, in specially built glasshouses, row upon row of orchids sit in carefully controlled conditions; they're not just there for their floral beauty, they also form a significant scientific collection of plants that are becoming increasingly rare in their natural habitats. Orchid enthusiasts from all over the world travel to Kew to visit the collection by special arrangement, and the plants are scrutinized by students and scientists alike.

Managing the collection for maximum impact during the festival is a delicate operation. It's not hard to ensure that there are enough orchids; thanks to modern micropropagation techniques, a single seed pod can reliably produce thousands of plants, with a near 100 per cent germination rate. What can't be controlled, however, is the exact time that they will flower. The team works towards mid-February, but natural conditions (a particularly cold or dark winter, for instance) sometimes mean that the plants don't flower in time. There have been occasions when a particularly spectacular orchid has been advertised as a star of the festival, and has then refused to perform on time. Orchids are no respecters of deadlines.

ABOVE: Kew's annual orchid festival is the perfect opportunity for the public to get up close to these exotic plants.

OPPOSITE: To boost Kew's reserve collection, orchids from specialist nurseries in Holland and Singapore are shipped in and mounted on pillars and huge display structures.

During the summer and autumn, the display team is busy developing the designs that will show the collection off to maximum effect. The orchid festival – which celebrated its tenth anniversary in 2004 – has become such a highlight of Kew's calendar that there's increasing pressure to come up with a concept and design earlier and earlier in the year, so that the marketing department can get out and sell the show to potential investors. On a more practical level, a decision has to be made about how much of the Princess of Wales Conservatory to give over to the festival. The available space in the conservatory is arranged around 16 permanent pillars; some of these are fully planted, while others can be stripped back to

make way for temporary displays. Staging the festival without disrupting the conservatory's regular inhabitants is a delicate operation.

The festival takes up about 2500 square metres (26,900 square feet) – and into that space the team stuffs thousands of individual orchids. Plants from the reserve collections are used exclusively for the species displays in the tropical and temperate zones. Plants bought in from Holland and 6500 cut stems from Singapore are mounted on pillars and display structures. The cut stems last seven to ten days, depending on the weather outside, and have to be replaced with new deliveries three or four times during the festival. Installing and maintaining the display is an enormous task that takes up all the energies of the team. Before they can work on the display, however, the reserve collections have to be boosted with fresh supplies from Dutch orchid nurseries. Every year Griffiths and Ruddy set off with a shopping list. They have to time their visit early enough to ensure they can get the appropriate flower colours and accurate dates of delivery, and to avoid the increase in orchid prices that takes place before St Valentine's Day.

OPPOSITE: The orchid displays look particularly splendid in late winter sunshine. If the weather is good, however, the cut stems from Singapore have to be replaced more frequently.

The orchid festival is the biggest annual event in the glasshouses; and, even though it's an expensive, delicate and labour-intensive operation, it has become a key part of Kew's annual planning – one that attracts the public at a time of the year when there isn't otherwise a great deal to see. The trees are bare and bulbs are only just starting to come out; it's cold and the weather is unreliable. But visitors to the festival know it will give them a big burst of colour, and that the glasshouses are always warm and dry. The orchid festival marks the real start of the year at Kew.

MANAGING THE GLASSHOUSES

PHIL GRIFFITHS
Displays Coordinator
of the Great
Glasshouses and
Training Section

My job mainly involves the display collections and structures at Kew, which need a huge amount of maintenance. They glasshouses are old structures, and they get very dirty, and it costs a fortune to keep them in good repair. As manager of all the public glasshouses – the Princess of Wales Conservatory, the Palm House, the Temperate House and a few satellite glasshouses – it's my responsibility to worry about them. Some of the wood in the Temperate House is so crumbly, it's like cheese. It was replaced a few years ago with softwood, because it's so much cheaper, but it rots a good deal quicker than hardwood, so it will have to be done again. But it's never as bad as I think. Recently I went to a conference in Sheffield about conservatories, and I met some guys from a company that specializes in the restoration of old bespoke Victorian glasshouses, and they told me that the problems we have at Kew are fairly minor. That put my mind at rest a bit; at least the glasshouses aren't going to tumble down around our ears.

Having said that, they're real money pits. You think your own house is a money pit, but these are worse. We've just refurbished a door at the north end of the Palm House, near the Waterlily House, and it took us the best part of a year and £6500 to get it right. If we do the same to the four big doors on either side of the Palm House, that could cost us £25,000 per door. The cleaning bills are huge as well, because it all has to be done by hand. These are unique buildings, and there's no machinery that can automate the cleaning process, like you might see on a modern glass building. If you're cleaning the Palm House, you're talking about a bloke up a cherry picker with a scouring pad on the end of a pole. It takes ages, and as soon as it's finished it needs doing again.

One of the best things about Kew being named a World Heritage Site is that I hope it will bring us a lot more money from corporate sponsorship, and that's something we really need if we're going to keep the glasshouses running properly. I believe it's going to take something in the region of £8 million to refurbish the Palm House completely, and there's just no way we can afford to do that at the moment. It would probably be less expensive to build new houses in modern materials that are easier and cheaper to maintain, but that would cause an outcry. My main concern is for the plant collections within each structure, which need to be looked after every single day and night. If a glasshouse experiences a major heating problem and we have just one cold winter night without heat, the effect on many of the tender plants would be disastrous.

BELOW: In order to best protect the Temperate House's plant collection, the world's largest surviving Victorian glass structure has to be kept in good condition.

One thing that certainly will be changing in the next few years is the way that the collections are presented in the big glasshouses. At the moment I think they're overstuffed; you literally can't see the wood for the trees. The Temperate House, for instance, can look dark and dull, and we need to make some tough decisions about what are the main plants. If we're not focusing on the important things, and just clogging the house up with a lot of rubbish, then we're not doing our job properly. Over the last two years, David Cooke, the unit manager of the Temperate House, has really started focusing on the collections and you can see the difference now. The glasshouses serve a dual purpose: they're scientific collections, but they're also spectacles in themselves. We've got to pull in the visitors by giving them something really interesting to see and the emphasis has to be on telling stories. As far as I'm concerned, the role of the glasshouses is purely educational, and if you're not getting people to go in there and really look, then you're not going to teach them anything. Kew has to be much more than just a scientific library of plants.

The same applies to the Palm House. You walk in there and have an overall impression of a dense, green, jungly planting. It's pleasant to walk through it, but it's hard for most people to see anything. So what if we've got an incredibly rare Madagascan palm, one of only two left in the world – how would anyone ever know? It's buried. I think we have to thin out those plantations so that the plants can be seen, and we need better, more interesting interpretation that will help visitors to engage with the displays.

One of the strategies we are introducing in the Temperate House is to try putting more stuff into containers and moving them outside during the summer. The climate is warm and dry enough to do that these days: certainly our citrus collection will thrive outdoors, as long as we can bring it indoors in the winter. That will clear a lot of space in the glasshouse, allowing more light to get in to the things that need it. At the moment it's so crowded in there that we're getting a lot of problems with pests and diseases. If we can clear some over-planted areas a little, then we'll be more able to control those things and the plants will all be healthier. As it is we lose a lot of light in the Temperate House because of dust and muck on the outside of the glass, and algae on the inside; we can't clean

Pagoda Tree *Sophora japonica*

LOCATION: West of the Princess of Wales Conservatory

DID YOU KNOW: This tree is one of the strangest at Kew. It twists and turns in almost every direction in a mass of horizontal and vertical growth. But the pagoda tree has every right to be a little eccentric – it's one of the original 1762 plantings, and as such qualifies as one of the garden's 'old lions'. Like its contemporaries, it originated from the estate of the Duke of Argyll, in nearby Twickenham, and was planted in the new arboretum by Lord Bute, the nephew of the duke and botanical adviser to Princess Augusta.

The pagoda tree's survival is little short of a miracle, as over the years it's been subjected to just about every treatment the arboricultural team could throw at it. The lower branch system has been propped, braced and bolted, and major cavity work was carried out on the main trunk in 1996, while new brickwork around the base has been constructed to provide extra support and protection.

every pane of glass every day, and the level of radiation naturally falls. But we can counteract that by thinning the plantings out and giving what's left a greater chance to thrive.

The palm collection is in serious need of rejuvenation as well. The trouble with palms is that, sooner or later, they're going to outgrow a conservatory. In the Temperate House we've got the biggest conservatory plant in the world in there, the big *Jubaea*, but sooner or later someone's going to have to grasp the nettle and take it down. It's just too big for its environment, and there's nothing else we can do. We've got other jubaeas growing up alongside it, and we're always bringing on new plants from seed – but that one is too big. People say to me, 'Oh that's awful, can't you dig it up and take it down to the Eden Project?' But we can't get it out of the building! We would have to take the entire roof off! It's not an endangered species, it's just very big. Someone suggested I could do something with a couple of Chinook helicopters – but they don't understand how heavy that plant is. Every 2 metres (6½ feet) of trunk probably weighs something like a ton.

My job often involves taking a collection and bringing it up to scratch. I looked after the orchid collection here at Kew for a while, which unfortunately had got a bit run down. Now, however, we've got the orchids in our new nurseries and the collection is coming back to life – we've got something like 5000 individual plants now, and it's growing all the time, thanks to help from outside. Kew has always been famous for its orchid collection; now I hope we're getting back to something we can be proud of. There's still a couple of empty spaces in the nursery that should be dripping with orchids – but I'm sure that, given time, they'll be full. And to keep the other collections going we need replacement plants coming through all the time. Sometimes plants outgrow their

space or we have to pass new material that's coming into flower to the Herbarium for verification and naming. Some plants we aren't able to get any more for various reasons, so we pollinate to produce seed, and even swap pollen with other international gardens.

It's important for Kew to give access to specialist groups, because they're the people who can really help us to develop skills we don't currently have. There's so much to look after at Kew that it's hard to become a real expert in one thing – so when you have someone who does nothing else but grow slipper orchids coming in to see you, you need to take advantage of that. Visitors always expect us to be specialists in everything. What we can do is share our resources with other groups and institutions. We're lucky enough to have a huge botanical holding here, and we have to share it with other people who need it. You can't just nip down to South Africa any more and help yourself to any plant you fancy – there are much stricter controls in place now, and it's right that there should be. Botanical gardens need to communicate with each other a lot more, to find out what they've got and what they need. A lot of my job is to do with bridge-building; it's something I feel very strongly about, because in the past Kew has tended to operate in isolation. We can't afford to hold ourselves apart from other institutions, because we're all working towards the same end.

ABOVE: As Kew's newest public glasshouse, the Princess of Wales Conservatory is somewhat easier to look after than the older structures. It still requires a great deal of maintenance, however, to allow light to filter through to the plants.

MARCH

The leaves are appearing on the trees, cloaking Kew in green lace as the first of the warm spring days bring the gardens to life. The birds are busy nesting and feeding and, if the weather's kind, the first of the spring butterflies, brimstones and peacocks will emerge from hibernation. For the garden staff, this is the time to get things ready for the big spring push. Roses are pruned and fertilized, herbaceous beds are mulched and planted up and, throughout the gardens, the lawn-mowers make their first appearance. And they'll keep mowing and mowing right through the year, until drought or frost prevents them.

This month at Kew, don't miss

- The spectacular crocus carpet early in the month
- Daffodils lining the Broad Walk
- Camellias between Victoria Gate and the Marianne North Gallery
- Spring bulbs throughout the gardens
- Spring bedding in front of the Palm House
- Cherry blossom on Cherry Walk
- Primroses and ladies' smock in Bethlehem Wood, Wakehurst Place

OPPOSITE: The blooming of Kew's famous crocus carpet surrounding the Temple of Bellona is a welcome sign that spring has arrived.

STUDENT VEGETABLE PLOTS

The 14 first-year students at Kew's School of Horticulture don't spend all their time in the lecture theatre: in October they take possession of their vegetable plots, which are situated behind the Order Beds. Each one gets a bed, roughly 30 square metres (320 square feet) in size, on which to raise a succession of crops throughout the year. It's not just an exercise in food production: the students are assessed at every step of the way.

BELOW: The Student Vegetable Plots present a good opportunity for visitors to interact with the gardeners and also to get ideas for what to grow at home.

When the beds are handed over they still contain the remnants of last year's vegetables, and can look a bit bedraggled. So the first task for their new stewards is to clear out all the old plants, then set about preparing the soil for crops. Compost from the vast heaps at the Stable Yard is dug in at the end of the year, and the students are assessed on how thoroughly and evenly they have done this. Winter weather will do the rest, as frost and rain break the soil down and, hopefully, introduce a good deal of moisture into the ground in time for the growing season.

The next task is to plan the use of the plot. Each student produces his or her design, alongside a sowing calendar that should maximize the use of the available space to produce as much food as possible in a year. There's a prescribed list of seeds that can be used. Some are obligatory (like courgette, radish, cabbage, carrot, onion, lettuce and spinach seeds) and others are optional (including climbing bean, cucumber, pea, turnip and tomato). A third group of decorative or complementary plants can also be used to improve the appearance and performance of the bed; these include antirrhinums, cosmos, chrysanthemums, sweet peas and French marigolds. It's important to use these plants wisely because the plots have to be entirely chemical-free: no chemical fertilizers, no herbicides and no pesticides. Certain plants can help keep pests at bay, and are useful weapons in the gardener's arsenal.

The Student Vegetable Plots used to be tucked away out of public view, behind the Herbarium; now, however, they can be seen by everyone and in recent years they have become a popular visitor attraction. This means they have to look good as well as turning out a high crop yield, so marks are given for appearance and presentation. In fact, the plots have become one of Kew's most interactive areas. Visitors like to engage the gardeners in conversation, exchanging information about vegetable husbandry, and hopefully taking home a few ideas about sustainability, recycling and natural pest-control.

Once the students have designed their gardens they start raising the crops upon which their final results will depend. Sowing begins under glass in February, and planting out starts around late March or early April depending on the weather. And this is when things really get busy: the students have to get as much food out of the ground as they can, which means successional sowing of fast-growing crops like lettuces or radishes, as well as careful maintenance of the slower yielders like carrots or turnips. In July, an external examiner marks each plot on a range of criteria including presentation, pest control, utilization of space and crop protection. This is the big event of the year – and it's the assessment upon which the most marks rely.

Good marks aren't the only reward for all this hard work – the students are allowed to keep and eat everything they raise, which is handy for those on a limited budget. Even though the plots are relatively small each yields more than one person can eat, if it is properly managed, so there's plenty of fresh produce to be had in Kew at the height of the season. Nothing goes to waste. Students sell excess crops at events held in the gardens, to raise money for their study trips; and, of course, anything that's left in the ground at the end of the growing season is taken straight back to the compost heaps to produce mulch for the next batch of keen vegetable gardeners.

FELLING THE BEECH TREE

Plants, like animals, have an allotted lifespan, and when their time's up they've got to go. In a managed environment like Kew it's not enough to allow trees to die and fall as they would in the wild – especially with so many visitors walking through the gardens every year. So when a tree has reached the end of its life, it has to be taken down and disposed of in the most environmentally friendly way possible. It's an important part of the annual cycle in Kew; if a tree has to be taken down, the arboricultural unit (or tree gang) generally aims to do it during the winter months.

This is what happened to a big old beech tree in the south end of the gardens in 2003. It was 24 metres (80 feet) tall and about 170 years old – most beeches at Kew have a life expectancy of about 120 years – and it was dying. After it had been identified as a potential hazard it was put on to the tree gang's winter work schedule, and it was up to the team leader, Jon Hammerton, to take it down. He started by climbing to the top of the beech to assess the state of its limbs and find out if they were sound enough for him to put ropes round them. A rope and pulley system is used to lower cut wood to the ground, so any branch that's chosen to be a roping axis has to be strong enough to bear weights of over a ton. The other end of the rope is secured to a tree about 90 metres (100 yards) away; this forms a 'speedline' that will lower the cut wood quickly and safely to the ground, carefully controlled by the rest of the tree gang at ground level.

When the ropes had been secured, Hammerton set about delimbing the beech with his chainsaw – a mighty piece of machinery with a 90-centimetre (35-inch) bar – starting at the top of the tree. Before each chunk was cut off it was secured with a rope. Then, when the cut had been made, it was speedlined away from the tree and, most importantly, away from Hammerton and his saw! Speedlining is a skilled job; if a branch is twisted or rotten, as is often the case with old trees, it may not fall straight and could knock an inexperienced feller off his perch.

Once a tree has been delimbed there are different options for getting rid of the trunk. If the tree is on its own, well away from glasshouses or other plants, the area is fenced off and it is felled in the normal way, with one cut near the base.

In the case of the old beech, however, there were other plants nearby, so it had to come down piece by piece. The trunk was divided into 2.4-metre (8-foot) sections, each of which was secured with ropes and plates, then Hammerton made a carefully positioned cut under the topmost section and the rest of the tree gang winched the cut block up and away from the tree. The process was repeated with the remaining sections.

The tree gang's job was over – but it wasn't the end of the story for the beech tree. A stump-grinder removed everything that had been left under the surface of the ground, while a chipper cleaned up all the leaves and smaller branches or 'brush'. The branches and sections of trunk were taken back to the Stable Yard, where the tree entered a new phase of its life. The largest parts of the trunk went through a

PLANT OF THE MONTH

Crocus *Crocus*

WHERE TO SEE THEM: Between the Victoria Gate and King William's Temple

DID YOU KNOW: The famous 'crocus carpet' at Kew comprises over one million plants of *Crocus vernus* cultivars, in shades of mauve, purple and white. It's one of the greatest sights of the year – but by no means the only crocus display of note in the gardens. Throughout the arboretum there are countless patches of the delicate lilac/purple *C. tommasinianus*, which are particularly beautiful along the Princess Walk. Both at Kew and at Wakehurst Place other crocus are happily naturalizing, including the familiar golden yellow *C. chrysanthus*.

BELOW: An Emily Young sculpture carved in marble. Some exhibits are mounted on recyclable material, such as wood from felled trees.

planking saw to make basket stakes to support the next generation of young trees. The 'scaffold' – the big, structural branches that form the main body of a tree – was cut into chunks to form display plinths for the Emily Young sculptures around the gardens. And suitable pieces of branch were incorporated into stag-beetle loggeries in the Natural Areas. The brush that had gone through the chipper was added to the compost heaps, whence, after a few weeks, it returned to the soil of Kew.

CARING FOR THE TREES

We have around 14,000 trees in Kew, so there's a lot of work for the arboricultural unit, or the tree gang as we're more commonly known. As the team leader I help to organize the work we're going to do; we get a list of aboricultural jobs that need to be done from Roger Howard, our line manager, and we prioritize the jobs we know are really urgent. The gang reports to the Stable Yard where we're based, we get equipped with chainsaws and other equipment and then we go out and climb trees. It's very rare that a day goes by when we are not up a tree in some part of the garden. In the summer there's a lot of pruning to be done; in the autumn and winter we have to do all the mulching, and bigger jobs like taking trees down. On top of that there's some indoor work in the glasshouses; if anything involves climbing or heights, they call in the tree gang, because we've got a head for it.

JON
HAMMERTON
Team Leader for the
Arboricultural Unit

We have to give individual attention to all the trees in Kew, and that means our job is endless. When we climb a tree, we're not only going up there to prune a branch; we're going to give that tree a full check-up, see if there are any weaknesses or disease, see if there's anything we can do to make the tree safer or prolong its life. A lot of the older trees are supported and held together with cables, whereas outside of a botanical garden those trees would probably just be felled. We've got trees that have been here since the very beginning of Kew, over 200 years old, and some of them really wouldn't survive without a bit of help. We get to know those trees very well indeed and we really love them. I can't go past them without going up and giving them a hug. There's a huge chestnut-leaved oak, over 30 metres (100 feet) high and 30 metres (100 feet) across. It's one of our biggest broadleaved trees, and it's something you really need to touch. The branches are as big as most trees you see out in the street. I take a lot of students round the gardens, and some of them just stand around looking at it. I always say 'Go on! Touch it! Feel it!'. People are always making jokes about tree-huggers, but to me it just seems like the most natural thing in the world.

Our job's very different from tree work in the outside world. A regular commercial tree surgeon wouldn't do all that work to support a limb; if it was weak, it would be dangerous to the public, and it would be taken off. I try to avoid taking wood down as much as possible. I'm not knocking commercial tree work; they're working in a very different environment. But mostly they just end up pollarding trees, whereas we have a chance to cherish them.

No matter how much we look after a tree, though, there comes a time when you have to cut off a limb or take the whole tree down. They don't last for ever. In the great storm of 1987 we had five or six beautiful old trees that lifted slightly out of the ground, and we had to make a very hard decision to take them out as they posed too much of a risk to the visitors. That storm was terrible – we lost about 700 mature trees in all, and the yard was full of trunks, while the rest of the gardens were just covered in matchwood. Everyone was very disheartened, but it was nature's way of thinning out the gardens and making room for new plantings, which we really needed. We started cleaning up at the north end and just went systematically through the garden, taking out everything that needed to go. Then in 1990 it happened all over again. In the 1987 storm, we lost all broadleaved trees, great oaks that you never thought would have come down. The wind came through and just pushed them over. In 1990 it was mostly conifers. It was a different sort of wind, swirling more; it got under the trees and twisted them out of the ground.

But we lose trees every year, and even though it's sad you learn that it's part of the natural process of things. Old trees make way for new trees, and the wood that comes down has a new part to play, whether it's used as posts around the garden, in the stag beetle loggeries, as plinths for sculptures or shredded and turned into mulch. Nothing's wasted.

If a tree has to come down, I like to be the one that does it. We've got some very good winching equipment now that you can attach to a branch or a section

of trunk, then I climb up to the top with my rope, make the cut and wood will be swung away from me and lowered safely to the ground. You have to know what you're doing; if a tree has got rot in it, a branch or section of trunk might fall in a different direction than you'd expect, and if you're up there with a 90-centimetre (35-inch) chainsaw you don't want a big chunk of wood suddenly swinging towards you.

ABOVE: *In the great storm of 1987, Kew lost about 700 mature trees and Wakehurst Place lost thousands, almost 40% of its entire tree collection.*

People are always saying to me, 'You must be really fit and strong to do your job,' but I'm not really – I haven't got big muscles. It's all about technique, really, and that's something that you can only learn on the job. Climbing a tree is something you can't learn from a book. You have to jump on to the trunk and throw yourself up. We have people coming here from horticultural colleges, or on the Kew Diploma Course, and they haven't got a clue how to get up a tree. The only way to learn is by experience.

When I was starting out I had a couple of tumbles. Years ago I was taking a sycamore down; I was coming down to the ground, and my rope looped itself off the fork I'd attached it to, and I fell about 3 metres (10 feet). Luckily I landed in a pile of brush, so I wasn't too badly hurt. When I first started I was learning to climb with Andy, who's been on the tree gang for 21 years, and I was leaning across a gap to get to another branch and I got stuck. My feet were gripping on to one branch, my hands were holding on to another, and there was nothing in between. I started panicking a bit, so Andy came up behind me and said, 'Oh come on!' and kicked my feet away so I just swung. That's how you learn to trust your rope. I would never have been able to do that for myself, but nowadays I spend all the time swinging around in the tops of trees and I think absolutely nothing of it.

Oriental plane *Platanus orientalis*

LOCATION: West of the Orangery

DID YOU KNOW: When the oriental plane was first introduced into Britain from southeast Europe in the sixteenth century there was some doubt as to whether or not it would flourish in the colder northern climate. When this specimen was planted at Kew in 1762 – making it one of the garden's 'old lions' – it was positioned at the corner of the old royal palace, or White House, just in case it needed protection from the elements. In fact, planes have proved to be one of the most successful imported trees, flourishing all over the UK and highly tolerant of heat, cold, drought and pollution – hence the success of the oriental plane's London cousin which, like all planes, shrugs off soot and dirt by permanently shedding its bark, enabling it to breathe easily in the dirtiest of atmospheres.

This particular platanus wasn't doing too well until recently, when decompacting the soil around its root base gave it a new lease of life.

I got into tree work completely by chance. I grew up in a village called Ham, not far from here. I left school at 16, I was bumming around, doing a bit of roofing – obviously I always had a head for heights! – but I didn't know what I wanted to do with my life. To be honest I was only interested in getting into trouble, and I was turning into a right little gangster. Then one day, by chance, I met Roger; I got to know him and after a while he asked me if I fancied coming and climbing trees for a living. It didn't really appeal much at the time; I was a spotty little teenager, and I wasn't interested in plants or gardens. But the money was better than anything else on offer, so I gave it a go – and I've been here for 17 years.

I can't say that I instantly fell in love with tree work; for the first five years or so I was a bit bored and restless. But then it just clicked with me. I started to feel that I was getting good at what I was doing, and I realized I'd fallen in love with the trees. I understood what they mean in the world, that they keep us alive, that they keep the planet breathing.

I never dreamed as a kid that this is what I'd end up doing with my life, but I wouldn't change it for anything. I've got the best job in the world and I live in Richmond Park. Kew set me up in life in so many ways; I don't know how I'd have turned out if I hadn't met Roger. The people here are like a family to me, and I hope I can pass some of that tradition on to another generation. Roger's dad worked at Kew and I'm hoping that when Roger retires I'll get a chance to step up to his job and carry on the tradition. We'll have about 100 years between the three of us. I'd like to take on another school leaver, someone like I was at 16, and bring him on. My oldest son says he wants to come and work at Kew, so we'll see; I'd like him to look at all the options first, rather than just following his dad.

Kew has a way of grabbing you, and once it's got you, it's got you for life. That's why so many people stay here for a long time. You either leave after a couple of years, or you're here for life. I've often thought about moving on, but where would I go? For someone who loves trees, Kew is the place. I just hope I'm lucky enough to spend the rest of my working life here.

APRIL Spring is well and truly sprung.

Throughout the woods and in the formal plantings there's a riot of colour. The birds are nesting, taking advantage of the longer, warmer days to rear their first chicks; if you're lucky, you'll see wrens in the ivy round King William's Temple and grebes performing their extraordinary mating ritual on the lake. Clouds of butterflies – tortoiseshells, commas, speckled woods and holly blues – emerge to flutter through the trees and bushes. And if you close your eyes around the great rhododendron plantations, you can smell the essence of spring long before you see the vast acreage of blooms.

This month at Kew, don't miss
- The Rhododendron Dell
- Magnolias throughout the gardens
- The Woodland Garden in full flower
- Magnolias and *Pieris* in the Slips, Wakehurst Place
- Spring bedding in the Pleasaunce, Wakehurst Place
- Rhododendrons in Westwood Valley, Wakehurst Place

OPPOSITE: In early April, the daffodils enjoy their final days of glory. As the weather turns milder, plants are bursting into flower all over Kew.

CUTTING THE BAMBOO

The glasshouses present special challenges to the tree gang, who are more at home in the open air where there are no large windows to break. But there are certain plants in the Temperate House and the Palm House that require their special skills on a regular basis – plants that grow so fast they could, if left unchecked, smash through the glass roofs of the buildings.

Cutting the giant bamboo in the Palm House is the toughest job of all. It's one of the fastest-growing plants in the world, and can put on over a foot in height every day – which makes it a great plant economically, but not the most convenient inhabitant for a Victorian glasshouse. Once the bamboo reaches the top of the Palm House roof it starts to grow along the inner surface of the glass, but there comes a point at which it is no longer content to bend and mould itself to the shape of the building, and it starts trying to push through the glass to the sky. Bamboo is strong stuff, and can easily pierce a man's flesh, so glass poses absolutely no challenge at all. Ideally, the top of the plant should be level with the Palm House walkway so that visitors can get a good view of its growing habit – and so, when it reaches a critical height, there's nothing for it but to bring in the arboricultural unit, or tree gang as they're more commonly known, to check its progress.

Heights aren't a problem for the tree gang; they're used to scaling the tallest trees in the garden. But while trees have convenient, sturdy branches, the giant bamboo offers nothing other than a smooth, flexible stem, which is not only hard to grip but which can also act as a kind of giant spring. If it's tackled in the wrong way, the tension in the stem can flick the unwary climber off his perch – and in an environment as full of glass as the Palm House, that's not such a great idea.

The architecture of the Palm House adds to the complications. Unlike the Temperate House, which has plentiful interior beams and high-level walkways, the Palm House is, in effect, a large glass dome. The walkway is about 12 metres (40 feet) from the ground and Jon Hammerton, team leader for the arboricultural unit, had to rely on his roping skills to get him into the roof area from there. He tied a sandbag to the end of a rope, then threw it from the walkway up into

OPPOSITE: Both the Palm House and the Temperate House contain fast-growing plants, like this giant bamboo, that require regular pruning to stop them smashing through the glass roofs of the buildings.

PLANT OF THE MONTH

Barrenwort *Epimedium*

WHERE TO SEE IT: Woodland Garden

DID YOU KNOW: Although it's not one of the most familiar plants in the spring garden, the *Epimedium* is fast establishing itself as one of the most attractive. It's good in dry shade, and is spreading well throughout the woodland areas, covered in exquisite blooms in the spring and attractive foliage for the rest of the year. There are more spectacular April flowers than the barrenwort – it's the time of peonies and tulips, after all – but this gentle woodland plant is without doubt a rising star.

the top of the Palm House and over a metal beam. There was only about a 15-centimetre (6-inch) gap between the beam and the glass roof, but he got the sandbag through without any breakages. The weighted rope was fed back down to the team on the ground and, safely secured to them in case of accidents, Hammerton swung across the open space into the body of the giant bamboo.

Once he had reached the bamboo canes, he gripped on 'like a koala bear' and started to hoist himself up to the very top of the plant. It was a difficult climb and downright unpleasant. The air at the top of the Palm House is always hot, even at seven o'clock in the morning when the job was done. Bamboo canes are also covered in fibres that cause a great deal of itching. And last but not least, the plants are havens for insects, particularly the cockroaches that enjoy the warm, humid conditions of glasshouses. So Hammerton, pouring with sweat, itching and crawling with bugs, made his way to the top of the giant bamboo and started cutting.

It came down in 1.8-metre (6-foot) sections; each chunk was roped off, cut and lowered carefully to the ground in order to protect the plant collections that flourish around the bamboo's base. The entire job was completed without incident, and Hammerton returned to the ground in one piece; it won't be long, however, before his bamboo-busting skills are in demand again.

Not all glasshouse jobs are quite so challenging. When the Chilean wine-palm (*Jubaea*) in the Temperate House started showing signs of distress, manager Dave Cooke called the tree gang in to have a look. The fronds of this palm have a limited lifespan, and when they die they turn brown and can easily be tugged off, leaving a neat scar on the trunk. This is part of the *Jubaea*'s natural life cycle, but Cooke was worried when a large number of fronds appeared to be folding down and dying. The tree gang climbed the palm, examined the fronds – and found the unmistakable marks of a squirrel's teeth. After a chase around the Temperate House the bushy-tailed offender was successfully removed from the building.

ABOVE: With so many tall plants in the Temperate House, the tree gang, for whom heights aren't a problem, are often called in to climb up high into the canopy.

MAINTAINING THE ARBORETUM

OPPOSITE: *The cherry trees in Kew's arboretum flower in late spring. Their delicate blossoms, in varying shades of pink and white, look their best against a deep blue sky.*

TONY HALL
Team Leader for
the Arboretum

I personally oversee all the work done on all the shrub collections plus all the young trees throughout the arboretum – and that covers about two-thirds of Kew Gardens, something like 80 hectares (200 acres). Alongside the maintenance of those plants – there are now about 1.5 million of them – I look after special projects like bulb planting in the autumn, tree planting, shrub pruning and so on. An arboretum is, literally, a garden of trees, and it's important that we keep Kew's collection in the best possible condition. After all, trees are what Kew is all about. I know that's not everyone's opinion, and certainly visitors tend to be more interested in the more obvious attractions like the glasshouses; the arboretum takes up the bulk of the gardens, but only gets about 50 per cent of the visitors. The crowds thin out as you penetrate deeper into the gardens, away from the Palm House and the main gates, the restaurants and the shops, and that's when you see Kew at its best. It's a peaceful, wild place, and you can often be completely alone with the trees.

I work very closely with the arboricultural unit, who deal with any treework above 4.5 metres (15 feet) – but I'm responsible for the overall maintenance of all the young trees and shrubs. That accounts for the vast majority of plants at Kew. There are lots of annuals in the formal plantings, but they're not going to be there for very long. Most of the things that last for any length of time are ours. You have to have a lot of patience in an arboretum, because you're not going to see instant results. We're always doing work that will benefit the plant a few years down the line; it's certainly not a job to do if you're looking for quick gratification. Even when we plant the bulbs in autumn, we have to wait for at least four months before we see anything – and even then they're not going to be at their best until they've been in the ground naturalizing for a few years. You develop a great deal of patience, working in a garden.

We do a lot of work on the younger trees, up to about ten years old, trying to make sure they grow into good, strong specimens. We call it 'formative pruning'; if a tree is growing with a double leader, for instance, that could cause problems in later life, so we'll prune out the weaker one and that gives the tree a better chance of growing straight and strong. We're not very interventionist; generally speaking we let nature take its course with the trees, because we want them to grow as naturally as possible, but there's a certain amount we can do to avoid the more obvious problems.

We're trying to develop the arboretum so that there's something of interest for visitors to look at all year round. Personally I think a tree is beautiful whenever you see it, whether it's completely bare in the winter or whether it's covered in leaves or blossoms throughout the rest of the year. But we add interest to the arboretum by using flowering shrubs and other plants – it's an effective way of pulling more visitors out through the garden, rather than just leaving them concentrated around the glasshouses.

The first flowers of the year, I suppose, are the camellias and the *Hamamelis* or witch hazels; they start flowering before Christmas, and they last well into spring. One of the best shows of the late winter is the *Hamamelis* with the snowdrops underplanted all around them. That's a planting scheme that I think works really well, because by the time the snowdrop flowers are going over the *Hamamelis* are coming into leaf, and you know that spring is really under way. Once the snowdrops have gone, the narcissi take over; we use 'February Gold', an early-flowering variety that really belts out the colour at the start of the season. People love daffodils, because they really seem to mark the change of the seasons.

By the end of February the crocus are coming into bloom, and that's certainly the most spectacular of all our bulb displays in the arboretum; they cover such a huge area, with the main focus round Victoria Gate and the Princess Walk. If you come into Kew that way during February and March, you'll be absolutely knocked out by the colour. Then in May it's bluebell time in the woods, which is another of our biggest visitor attractions, and my favourite of all the bulb displays.

After the bulbs, we get into the flowering shrub season, which is probably when the arboretum looks at its best. We've got a lot of viburnum and magnolia, but the real impact comes from the azaleas and rhododendrons in April and May. The azalea garden can be seen from all over the garden – but I have to say they're not my favourite plants. I think the colours are rather harsh, all those hot oranges and reds and yellows. I much prefer the rhododendrons. They flower for longer – the earliest rhododendrons are coming out in January, the latest last till October – so you really get your money's worth. And I like the colours; they're more muted, and they seem to go better with their own foliage somehow. The Rhododendron Dell is quite concealed, you can't see it from all over the garden, but once you get there in the height of the flowering season, in April and May, it's like walking into an enchanted world. The colours and the scents are overpowering.

Flowering shrubs take us right through to October, then there's a bit of a gap in November and December. Obviously the autumn leaves look pretty good at that time of year, so you'll never be short of colour in the arboretum, but I'd like to find something that will flower right through till the cycle starts again with the *Hamamelis* in December.

Generally speaking, our year divides into two sections: the autumn and winter, when we're doing all the hard work of bulb and tree planting and major renovation; and the spring and summer, which is our maintenance period when we prune, water and weed. It doesn't always work that way; in 2003, for instance, we had a terrible drought, and so most of our maintenance time was taken up

ABOVE: Kew's stunning azaleas and rhododendrons are one of the most popular attractions in April and May.

with irrigation and we got behind with all the regular work that needs to be done. We generally lose a few week and diseased trees and shrubs after a drought, but that's all part of nature's scheme. We lose a few things every year, but they're quickly replaced. We plant on average 100 new trees a year, so there's always as many going in as we take out.

I've worked with trees for a long time now. As soon as I left school I went to work for a tree surgeon, and after that I was with various landscaping firms before I went into business for myself for a while. It was during a slack period in my own business that I decided to go for a job at Kew; I've always lived near here, and I've visited it all my life, so I thought it would make sense to work here. A job came up as a paper-picker and I thought that would be a possible way in, so I applied. I got a letter back saying I was far too qualified to be a paper-picker,

TREE OF THE MONTH

False acacia *Robinia pseudoacacia*

LOCATION: East of the Orangery

DID YOU KNOW: Another of Kew's 'old lions', this venerable robinia owes its continued existence to the tender loving care of the tree gang over the last 20 years – left to its own devices it would have died. As the robinia grew over its 240-year life the main trunk died back and was replaced by new shoots – now mature trees in their own right – coming from the middle of the plant and the tree was in danger of falling to pieces. To prevent this, the giant bundle of wood is held together by metal bands, 15 centimetres (6 inches) wide, which run round its main body, while the heavy branches are supported by cables.

but that there was a nine-month contract doing bits and pieces in the arboretum. I said yes, of course – and within a year they gave me a full-time contract. I've been here for four years now, and I've been promoted twice in that time. My job used to be called senior botanical horticulturist, which is more or less like an old head gardener, but now it's been changed to team leader, which is much more in keeping with the management structures at Kew these days.

Now I've established myself at Kew I want to be here for ever. It's funny: I've always loved Kew, but I never thought I'd work here. After just three months, I knew it was the job for me. Kew has a way of getting to you, and now I hope this is the job I'll retire from.

Kew's a wonderful place. You can come through the gates at seven o'clock in the morning, long before the public comes in at half past nine, and it feels like you're walking into your own private garden. It's quiet, there are foxes and badgers running around, and even though you're only just off the main road you can barely hear the traffic, just a gentle hum in the background. I always take the longest possible route between the gate and the mess room in the morning, just so I can see the garden when it's quiet and empty. Nothing changes much from day to day, I suppose, but there are certain things that I have to see and check up on. It seems as though I've been here for 20 years already, I feel that closely involved with the gardens and the plants.

It's hard to say what my favourite time of year at Kew is. Autumn is wonderful: I hate the heat, and it's great when you feel that change in the air and you move into the cooler autumn weather, with the smell of fungi and dead leaves in the air. Winter can be a bit wet and dark, but we've always got plenty of work to do. I suppose spring is really my favourite time, when you get that first flush of green on the trees and the first splash of colour from the bulbs. In the winter you can pretty much look from one end of the garden to the other, but when the leaves come they divide Kew up into different areas, and there's a wonderful sense of mystery about it. It's always a joy to come into work here, whatever the weather is doing, but on a nice spring morning there really is a bit of magic in the air.

OVERLEAF: Judas tree blossom falling on the paths of the Queen's Garden behind Kew Palace adds a welcome touch of informal colour.

INVASION OF THE BEES

Bees are probably the most important animals in Kew. They're champion pollinators, working throughout the spring, summer and autumn to ensure that all the flowers have a fair chance of producing seeds. Bumblebees are particularly useful – they can fly in cold conditions, whereas honeybees need temperatures of at least 10°C (50°F) before they become active. Bumblebees, which are frequently solitary and live in holes rather than hives, are even seen pollinating snowdrops in the winter months.

But bees can sometimes be a curse rather than a blessing. One April, just before the Easter weekend – which marks the beginning of Kew's busiest period – and shortly before the annual bluebell festival was about to get under way, three clusters of honeybees appeared in a tree next to a path that passes the bluebell woods. They weren't Kew natives; they had most probably broken away from an overpopulated swarm in nearby hives, and decided to make a new home in the wide, open spaces of the gardens. But they were too close to public areas, and had to be dealt with.

Tony Hall is Kew's resident bee man as well as team leader for the arboretum. He keeps hives at home, and has brought some to the gardens to supplement the 'official' swarms, housed in the Queen's Garden. So he donned his bee suit and set about tackling the uninvited guests.

Destroying them was out of the question. Apart from anything else, a few extra bees in the gardens are good news for the plants, and increase the annual yield of Kew honey. So Tony was obliged to remove each of the three clusters from the tree,

BELOW: Bees are vital for pollinating Kew's plants. And they make a delicious honey, which is very popular among the staff.

snipping off the narrow branches the bees had settled on and dropping them carefully into boxes before relocating the insects in more suitable accommodation in Kew's hives. Fortunately for everyone, the bees agreed that their new home was preferable to the tree, and allowed the bluebell festival to proceed without incident.

Kew honey is much in demand among the staff (there isn't enough, even in a good year, to consider selling it to the public). In 2003, a lucky few enjoyed it spread on the first-ever Kew bread, made entirely from grain raised in the Go Wild! corn field. To produce this, 0.4 hectares (1 acre) of corn was sown using traditional hand-scattering methods, allowed to flourish without pesticides or weedkillers, and then harvested by scythe and hand-milled. The flour made a loaf of bread, which was spread with honey and scoffed in the arboricultural unit's messroom. Tony Kirkham, head of the arboretum at Kew, who oversaw the project, reckons the loaf cost about £4000, but was worth every penny.

ΛBOVE: The Kew staff often use traditional techniques and tools to gain a greater understanding of the plants and environments they work with. In 2003, the cornfield was scythed by hand and the harvested corn used to make Kew's first-ever loaf of bread.

MAY

At Kew, May is bluebell time, and the gardens celebrate with the Spring to Life Festival. With longer days and a decent promise of good weather, the visitor numbers are high, and the gardens are moving towards their summer splendour. The arboretum is now a sea of green, with the fully-clothed trees forming unexpected, secret spaces, hidden from view – a far cry from the bareness of winter. And around the water features the dragonflies and damselflies are emerging to begin their short but busy lives.

This month at Kew, don't miss

- Bluebells in the Queen's Cottage Grounds, Kew and Horsebridge Wood, Wakehurst Place early in the month
- The azaleas
- Lilacs near White Peaks
- Tiny but beautiful flowers in the Rock Garden, Himalayan blue poppies and rhododendrons in the Woodland Garden and native plants in the long grass areas
- Horse chestnut blossom
- Herbaceous plantings in the Water Garden, Wakehurst Place

OPPOSITE: The magnificient carpets of bluebells in Kew's Natural Areas and at Wakehurst Place are a reminder that this land was once natural woodland.

SUMMER BEDDING

The spring and summer bedding on the pond side of the Palm House is one of the great eye-catchers of Kew. In contrast to so much in the gardens, these are formal, highly designed, highly maintained plantings that have absolutely nothing to do with natural habitats, science or conservation – and absolutely everything to do with the visual rapture of colour, shape and size. They're the sort of borders we all dream of creating in our own gardens, and they look effortlessly elegant when they're at their abundant best. This, however, is a carefully contrived impression that belies months of planning and weeks of hard work.

The Palm House borders are planted twice a year: once in October for the spring display, and once in May–June for the big summer show. On each occasion, the entire decorative unit is pulled off individual jobs in the Queen's Garden, the Duke's Garden and so on, and is helped by other hardy display team members to get the plantings done in time. The backbreaking work takes place in October, when not only does all the summer bedding have to be removed, but the soil has to be dug over and refreshed as well. Many of the plants are still in flower, so it can be a heartbreaking task – and visitors regularly ask the gardeners why they're taking out something that's still looking so good. But the plants don't go to waste. Perennials will, by and large, go to specific collections in the gardens where they're needed, while annuals are frequently used as source material for cuttings that will be overwintered in the nurseries before being planted out again the following year. And, of course, anything that can't find a place in a bed or a nursery will be composted and returned to the garden as mulch.

Feeding the soil is an important autumn job. Kew's is notoriously thin and hungry, and the Palm House beds need a lot of help to sustain the massive demands made on them by a year's worth of bedding plants. So the soil is dug over and then enriched with well-rotted manure and mulch from Kew's own compost heaps. It's a big job, and it means the beds are empty for a few days – but without this annual feed, there wouldn't be a spring or summer display. Cleaning, digging, feeding and planting the Palm House borders for the spring display takes up all of October.

The planting is designed to provide some colour right through the cold, dark months with pansies and polyanthus, dependable winter performers, forming the backbone of the display. Tulip and hyacinth bulbs are planted densely throughout the beds to flower in the spring, guaranteeing one of the most dazzling sights in the Kew calendar. Each year's planting is designed round a simple colour scheme, such as yellow and red.

But it is the summer bedding that really brings out the showmanship of the decorative unit. Throughout the winter and spring, thousands of annuals and

BELOW: The formal summer bedding displays outside the Palm House are always vibrant and colourful and a big hit with visitors.

perennials are brought on in the greenhouses to create the extravagant designs that complement Kew's most famous building, and make the Palm House and its environs the unquestionable centre of the gardens.

It all starts with the design. In recent years, there has been a return to bold, clashing colours that create the maximum impact. In 2003, for instance, the dominant colours were orange and purple, and it looked as if the front of the Palm House was on fire. Deep purple heliotropes and *Gazania* sat next to brilliant orange *Tagetes* and the pink-orange, sherbet shades of begonias, all highlighted by dark foliage plants and grasses. The same colour scheme was repeated, in slightly muted tones, in the two 'roundabout' beds at either end of the Broad Walk. Under the blazing sun of what was an exceptionally hot summer, this was one of Kew's most memorable sights.

The design for 2004 is altogether less violent, celebrating the traditional English cottage garden. It contrasts the extreme formality of the Palm House beds, which are cut in precise geometric designs, with the informality of old-fashioned flowers like delphiniums. The dominant colour is again purple – but this time it's teamed with white, which is slightly easier on the eye.

Most plants in the Palm House borders are raised at Kew, from seed. A few perennials are bought every year, preferably ones that will find a home in other parts of the gardens after their starring role in the summer display, but this is an expensive and potentially wasteful way of filling up the borders. Seed is much cheaper – even though once the costs of labour, pots and growing medium are factored in, it's not a great deal less expensive than buying in ready-grown annuals from an outside nursery. But the raising of plants is an important part of the education and training programme at Kew; this is how the nurserymen and horticulturists of tomorrow learn their plant husbandry skills. It's also a good exercise for the senior gardeners who design the different displays each year. They have to create their effects with plants from seeds that are available from tried and trusted suppliers, and which will thrive well in the conditions at Kew. The summer display, in particular, has its origin in a handful of seed catalogues that are pored over every year for new inspiration.

THE NATURAL APPROACH

I worked with the arboricultural unit (or tree gang) for seven years, and during that time I became interested in a comparatively small part of the gardens, then known as Queen Charlotte's Cottage Grounds, which was quite different in appearance from the rest of Kew. Covering an area of 16 hectares (40 acres), the Cottage Grounds were given to Kew in 1897 by Queen Victoria in celebration of her Diamond Jubilee. It was her wish that this area should be retained and managed, not only for its flora, but also for the wildlife that found sanctuary there. Until recently the area wasn't really recognized and used as an educational resource for Kew and was definitely undervisited, except in spring, of course, when the bluebells were out. Over the years, many of the habitats that made the area so interesting for wildlife, such as the grassy, flower-rich meadows that support a broad range of dragonflies and butterflies, had slowly begun to revert back to scrub woodland. Of course woodland habitat is incredibly important in its own right, but if we sat back and watched all the grassy areas disappear under trees, the animal and plant species that thrive in the more open areas would disappear too. Other important habitats, such as the small gravel pit, dug in 1974 to extract gravel for the foundations of the Alpine House, had also started to revert to woodland, following years of unofficial dumping of waste soil and vegetation from the arboretum.

SIMON COLE
Manager of the
Natural Areas

Prior to my appointment as manager of the Cottage Grounds in April 2002, now known as the Natural Areas or the Conservation Area, this part of the gardens had never received any full-time management, although the tree gang usually spent a couple of weeks every year removing invasive exotic species. Therefore the post represented a fantastic opportunity for me to address the longer term issues of habitat management. During

my years with the tree gang I had tried to introduce a few ideas that were in line with my thinking on conservation. I was constantly moaning that we should convert timber felled in the gardens into tree-planting stakes instead of importing softwood stakes that probably originated from Scandinavia, which rot after a few years in the ground, and was forever leaving little log piles tucked away under bushes to create wildlife habitats.

I begin my day at half past seven and, in theory at least, finish at three fifteen, although I'm usually still here at five or six, depending on the time of year and what we've got on. My work hasn't turned out to be as hands-on as it was working with the arboricultural unit, which has taken some adjusting to. It is very varied though; one day I'm planning a new project or researching a subject, the next I'm installing new fencing or replanting the woodland. Then there are the requests from other departments for bundles of hazel coppice wood to support the runner beans in the students' vegetable plots or bits and pieces for the seasonal displays in the Princess of Wales Conservatory.

If I had to sum up the principle differences between the Natural Areas and the rest of the gardens, I would say that the main principles of management tend to be ecological (often untidy) compared to horticultural (tidy). It depends largely on how you view tidiness, I suppose; a weed in one place may not be a weed in another. Most gardeners, for instance, would regard a bramble as an invasive weed, but for me it's one of the most important plants in the Natural Areas.

Brambles are a valuable nectar and food source for all sorts of insects and birds and provide good nesting opportunities. It's the same with stinging nettles: while everyone else is clearing them away, I'm encouraging them because they're a great food source for a lot of caterpillars of many butterfly species. And it would be inappropriate to leave dead trees unfelled in the gardens for safety reasons, but we leave all the dead trees standing in the Natural Areas because of their ecological contribution to the habitat as a whole – they make a perfect home for fungi, insects and birds.

ABOVE: Kew's Treetop Walkway offers visitors a unique opportunity to interact with nature.

May

Bluebell *Hyacinthoides non-scripta*

WHERE TO SEE THEM: Natural Areas at Kew;
woodland at Wakehurst Place

DID YOU KNOW: There are few sights more breathtaking
than a British woodland with bluebells in full bloom,
and between them Kew and Wakehurst Place have two
of the best habitats in the UK. Bluebells are intimately
associated with ancient woodland, which covers two
per cent of Great Britain but is constantly threatened
by habitat destruction. The plants themselves are also
under threat, not from humans (it's illegal to pick them
without the landowner's consent) but from other
plants. The cultivated Spanish bluebell (*Hyacinthoides
hispanica*), with its upright flowering stems, is a garden
escapee that hybridizes easily with its British cousin,
thus diluting its genetic purity and stealing its habitats.

Public access to the Natural Areas is limited, because we treat it as a reserve and
restricting visitors allows us to minimize the effects of trampling and general
disturbance. I am hoping to increase visitor access in the future though, with an
interpreted nature trail that will thread its way through the woodland area.

A new project for 2004 is to build a large wildlife pond to attract amphibians
and dragonflies, which will complement the other wetland habitats in the area
– the gravel pit and a small woodland pond – both of which dry out in the
summer as a lot of natural ponds do. We'll have a pond-dipping platform shaped
like a lily pad that should encourage local schools to visit, facilitated by Kew's
public education team.

This marks a big shift of attitude in Kew, and an expansion of the whole idea of what a botanical garden can be. I always thought it was an anomaly that we had such wonderful global habitats represented at Kew – rainforests, deserts, even coral reefs – but we weren't paying attention to our own backyard habitats, such as woodland and meadows, and their ecosystems. That's all changed over the last five or six years though, which I think is a good thing. Recently we had a summer festival called Go Wild! that celebrated biodiversity in the UK. I was involved with some of the projects, such as the Treetop Walkway and the human-sized badger sett, which have proved to be very popular with visitors.

I see the Natural Areas as a giant classroom, where the visitor can observe plants and animals in a less formal setting. It worries me a bit that nowadays everyone seems to know the difference between a Ford Mondeo and a Ford Sierra, but how many people can tell the difference between an oak and an ash? And those trees are around us all the time, often right outside our front doors. The UK has a large but declining percentage of Europe's ancient trees, and they represent an enormously important cultural and biological resource, as well as a window into the past. I think the Treetop Walkway has allowed visitors to gain a new perspective on trees, as it gets people to interact with them in a very different way, 10 metres (33 feet) from the ground. The interpretation plaques along the way explain the key differences between deciduous oak trees and evergreen redwoods. As a species, the oak can support more than 450 different species of plant and animal – it surely must qualify as the heavyweight champion of British trees.

People have responded to the Treetop Walkway in a very positive way. It's been such a joy to see people's faces and gauge their reaction when they climb up. If I can get children up there and just encourage them to marvel at the trees, then that's an amazing step, because so many of the kids that come to Kew, especially those who live in London, never get the chance to get out into a British woodland. For many children, they're really meeting trees for the first time, and it has a big impact on them. School parties have visited and sent in poems and paintings about trees and how they feel about them, which we've displayed along the length of the walkway. It's surprising how stepping over an oak branch 9 metres (30 feet) up in the air can inspire you.

One of the key messages I want to get across to the visitor is that we can all contribute to biodiversity conservation – it's not something that should be left to land managers, park keepers and Kew gardeners. Many rural habitats have suffered serious decline and town gardens have become increasingly important in supporting a tremendous variety of plant and animal life. Over 1500 flowering plant species and something like 300 species of bird have been recorded in London in recent years. More people than ever before are moving into the city and the competition for space is fierce and often uncompromising, so it's vitally important that we all act now if we want to safeguard our urban wildlife heritage for the future.

I'd like people to come away from a visit to Kew with some practical ideas. They might think about leaving a few logs to decompose in a shady part of the garden to help support beetles and other insects or perhaps using some dead wood to build a stag beetle loggery. They might think about allowing the grass to grow long in one area to attract butterflies and encourage wildflowers to grow. They might want to put a pond in the garden – not just an ornamental pond with goldfish, but a real wild pond where frogs and newts can lay eggs and dragonflies can breed. I'd like people to think about planting more native species instead of relying on big showy hybrid blooms that are often very poor on nectar for bees. Don't be worried by the odd chewed leaf here and there; it means you've got some interesting visitors, and that's much better than a picture-perfect garden. And certainly be more conservative with pesticides that interrupt natural ecosystems if you can; encourage ladybirds and frogs that provide a more biological control. Be a little adventurous and creative in the garden and you'll be rewarded by your efforts.

I guess it brings us back to tidiness again and our interpretation of gardening principles. I hope that the work my colleagues and I are involved with will bring some of these issues into mainstream gardening practice, helping to safeguard many declining species for future generations to enjoy. I hope that's the message

Caucasian Elm *Zelkova carpinifolia*

LOCATION: Herbarium paddock

DID YOU KNOW: This is another of Kew's 'old lions', planted in 1762 only two years after *Zelkova carpinifolia* was first introduced to Britain in 1760. There were originally three specimens in the gardens but only the Herbarium tree remains. The other two were lost in the 1987 hurricane and the storms of 1990.

people take away from a visit to Kew. We've become so used to the idea of striving towards a perfect, neat, beautifully designed garden that I think we've lost sight of the fact that one of the most important functions of a garden is to provide an oasis for wildlife, and to maintain our threatened biodiversity. Gardening programmes are all very well, and if they inspire people to get their hands dirty that's a great thing – but I don't think they put nearly enough emphasis on nature conservation issues. It's all about decking and design and aluminium pots, none of which does anything to make your garden good for wildlife.

Kew is becoming greener and greener; we're tying up loose ends, using our own resources more so that nothing gets wasted. Felled timber isn't a disposal issue any more, for instance; now we've got the stag beetle loggeries, which I hope will spread across the garden, we've got wooden sculptures, we're using our own coppices to provide stakes, and everything else gets shredded and put on to the composting piles. I particularly like having the wooden sculptures around the gardens, because it's a way of emphasizing the fact that everything has a use, even after we think of it as dead. It just goes back into the circle of life in a different way. All these things are happening at Kew now, and if I can help to spread the greener gardening message, then I'm doing my job.

A BADGER SETT FOR HUMANS

A permanent, human-sized badger sett was built in the woodland conservation area in 2003 – new for Kew, and part of a wider policy of bringing visitors across the gardens from the 'honeypot' areas of the Palm House and Orangery, and out into Kew's wilder corners.

It's an extraordinary structure, based around concrete tunnels and chambers, which are covered over with earth and grass, and lined with organic materials such as wood bark and moss that give the closest possible approximation to the underground world of one of our largest, but least seen wild animals. Badgers were, until quite recently, a threatened species in the UK, but are on the increase now, with three or four family groups living in Kew. Visitors seldom see them, but they're doing well and raising families, despite setbacks in dry summers when cubs have been found starved because of the unavailability of earthworms, their preferred diet. But that's nature's way of keeping the population in check; overall, Kew's badgers are thriving.

Work on the sett started in January 2003, when an environmental design company started turning its designs into reality. The result is a green mound with tunnel-like entrances to sleeping rooms, dining areas and a nursing nest for the mothers. There are amusing interpretation signs and menu boards to add interest. The main customers are, of course, children, but the scale is big enough for human adults to get around without constantly bumping their heads, and the sett is wheelchair accessible.

It opened in May 2003, after some frantic all-night sessions putting in the finishing touches, and it has proved to be a massive draw to visitors – with all the problems attendant on this popularity. Children have naturally taken particular delight in dismantling things, unscrewing the wood bark from the walls, and breaking up displays and dropping them down the light tubes. Even the wooden sculptures of badgers that adorned the sett haven't been safe; they've been thrown around and lost the odd limb. It's been a challenge to keep up with the maintenance! Soil erosion has also been a problem, and the sett will need regular refurbishment if it's going to remain open. But, like the badgers it celebrates, the sett should be safe at Kew for years to come.

OPPOSITE: Kew's human-sized badger sett allows visitors to gain a new perspective on the lives of an animal that is a protected species in the UK.

JUNE

Think of an English garden and you think of June: the roses in full bloom, the herbaceous displays at their best, the bees working drunkenly from flower to flower. The birds are feeding furiously, and the native butterflies are joined by swarms of colourful migrants like Painted Ladies and Red Admirals. The gardeners can sit back and admire the fruits of their labours in June – but, in the hotter summers that we've been enjoying recently, it's also the time when they have to devote more and more of their energies to watering.

This month at Kew, don't miss

- Wonderful display of roses on the Rose Pergola and in the Rose Garden
- Summer flowers in the Duke's Garden and Woodland Garden
- Giant waterlilies growing fast in the Waterlily House and the Princess of Wales Conservatory
- Mediterranean plants near King William's Temple
- Magnificient floral display in the Order Beds
- Tulip trees, mock orange and hebes flowering throughout the gardens
- Giant Himalayan lilies, blue poppies and *Primula* in the Water Garden, Wakehurst Place

OPPOSITE: The spectacular laburnum arch in the Queen's Garden, with its hanging flowers, provides welcome shade in hot summer months.

LOGGERIES FOR STAG BEETLES

Most people over 30 who grew up in the southeast of England might well remember the stag beetle (*Lucanus cervus*) as one of the creepy-crawly stars of the playground and garden – particularly the adult male, up to 7 centimetres (2¾ inches) in length with a formidable pair of jaws. But populations have been declining over the last decade or so with the loss of their habitat – dead wood – and now the stag beetle is a threatened species, protected by the Wildlife and Countryside Act of 1981. No surprise, then, that Kew is doing its bit to save an animal that is as much an emblem of the British countryside as the oak tree or the robin redbreast.

Simon Cole, manager of Kew's Natural Areas, has been hoarding felled tree trunks and logs for years, with an eye to creating a large-scale habitat for stag beetles – and in 2002 the main loggery was built. An impressive structure, it comprises about 30 tree trunks and logs, buried 90 centimetres–1.2 metres (3–4 feet) deep in the earth, and standing about 3 metres (10 feet) tall, complemented by three smaller structures in front.

To appreciate why loggeries are necessary it's important to understand that the stag beetle's life cycle is dependent on decaying wood. Eggs are laid in soil at the foot of tree stumps or fence posts – wherever there is rotting wood. Once the eggs hatch they burrow down and start feeding on this wood – and remain in this state for up to seven years. A loggery therefore provides a habitat where adults can lay their eggs and larvae can feed.

Following pupation, stag beetles emerge as splendid, highly armoured adults and set about looking for a mate. They emerge from the ground from May to August, race to breed and, having done so, die. It is thought that a few adults may overwinter in warm locations like compost heaps, but for the vast majority their adult instar is a brief, glorious few months, even weeks in some cases.

It is the larvae, and not the adults, that are important to the environment. They may be unlovely but, hidden away under ground, they are doing sterling work in the decay process, breaking down dead wood so that nutrients return to the soil.

With the general move towards tidy gardens, stag beetles are losing their habitats at an alarming rate. Rotting wood is anathema to most gardeners, and the

former strongholds of these wonderful insects are now sparsely populated. Kew Gardens, however, is bucking the trend not only by creating the right habitats, but also by actively providing a home for larvae accidentally dug up in other parts of the garden.

The conservationists at Kew get a number of calls from people who have found stag beetles and don't know what to do with them. They encourage gardeners to leave them alone, because relocation can not only be bad for the beetles but can jeopardize local breeding. If, because of imminent habitat changes, any larvae found can't stay where they are, they can be relocated to Kew's loggery.

The loggeries are well established and are becoming a major visitor attraction – thanks, in part, to the giant wooden sculptures of stag beetles that romp around them. They have also excited a good deal of interest among fungi specialists and lovers of native fauna at Kew. Over 80 species of fungi were recorded on the main loggery in its first year, some of them new to the gardens, and one of them apparently previously unrecorded in European literature. Some of the logs were sourced from tree surgeons outside Kew, and contained latent fungal spores that contributed to the decomposition of the wood.

After all this effort, has it been worth it? Do the stag beetles repay the time and energy that's been put into building them a new home? The experts are in no doubt. Stag beetles are one of the great recyclers – without them the world

ABOVE: The stag beetle loggery, complete with giant wooden sculptures, is now well established at Kew. Conservationists are keen to encourage visitors to create similar loggeries in their own gardens.

would be more cluttered up with dead wood and there would be fewer nutrients in the soil. And apart from their usefulness they're among the most exciting animals in the garden, the biggest of the 3500 species of beetles in the UK – the Rolls-Royce of the insect world. Thanks to Kew, and to the gardeners who are following Kew's example, this magnificent beast, once so common in the south of England, may again flourish to delight future generations.

PLANT OF THE MONTH

Rose *Rosa*, various cultivars

WHERE TO SEE THEM: Climbing roses on the Rose Pergola in the Order Beds; shrub roses in the Rose Garden behind the Palm House

DID YOU KNOW: Kew's Rose Garden was created in 1923 (although the *Rosa hugonis* plants are nearly 100 years old) and comprises 54 beds, each containing a different kind of rose. All are selected for their suitability to British gardens and there's a huge variety to be seen: floribundas, hybrid teas, and shrub and Old English roses, with colours ranging from deep reds nearest the Palm House to yellows and whites near the perimeter of the Rose Garden, against green vistas and hedges.

The Rose Pergola, constructed for Kew's bicentenary in 1959, is one of the most striking features of Sir Joseph Hooker's Order Beds. The beds are a living library of plants, arranged to demonstrate to students the relationship between different groups, and the Pergola covers the central path. In June it's a mass of climbing roses in many different colours.

A TOUCH OF FORMALITY

I lead the teams who do the formal plantings in the Queen's Garden, the Duke's Garden, the bedding in front of the Palm House, the roundabouts at either end of the Broad Walk and one or two other bits and pieces. I have weekly meetings with all those responsible for the individual areas to make sure that all the gardens are covered by staff, that the right jobs are being prioritized and that we've all got the equipment we need. I try to be as hands-on as possible because I think it's important we all share our skills and train each other. Skill-sharing goes upwards as well as downwards in the Kew management structure; we've got people coming into certain areas with specialist knowledge, and everyone should learn from that. I know about herbaceous plants, for instance, but I'm not too good on pruning trees and shrubs; I'm always on the look-out for an opportunity to learn about that.

SARAH SMITH
Team Leader for the
Decorative Unit

As well as being a team leader, I'm also a manager of the Queen's Garden, so that's the real focus of my work. I moved over from the Duke's Garden in 2002, and had to learn a lot of new skills very quickly. The Queen's Garden lies behind Kew Palace (built in the 1630s), which George III lived in, and we've tried to make it historically authentic. All the plants we grow here were grown in England in the seventeenth century, and the design elements are true to the styles and fashions of the day. At the back of the house an avenue used to run down to the river, surrounded by meadows on either side that were prone to flooding. In 1969, following an earlier suggestion by the Duke of Edinburgh, a formal garden was put in to complement the royal associations of the palace.

The main feature of the garden is the parterre, which is a series of box hedges enclosing planted pockets. We've mixed shades of grey and bronze foliage – there's a lot of *Santolina*, lavender, sage and *Heuchera*, and a few other plants that we grow for foliage rather than flowers. But I think it's all going to be dug up fairly soon. The palace is being opened to the public in 2006 and I want the garden to be absolutely pristine for that. It's got to look good from above, so that when visitors look out of the upstairs window they'll see a really stunning design. We can't take the box hedges out, because they're expensive and very slow to grow, but we're

ABOVE: The formal
plantings and
box hedging in the
Queen's Garden,
which accurately
reflect seventeenth-
century gardening
practice, require
a great deal of
maintenance by
Sarah Smith and
her team.

going to go for something more striking in the planted pockets. The plants in there now are getting a bit tatty, and they look a bit bland. I want something that's going to hit you in the eye and make you go 'Wow!' when you look down on it.

As well as the parterre, we've got a number of other authentic seventeenth-century features. There's a shaded walk of hornbeam, which was important in the period because it was fashionable for ladies to have very pale skin, so they needed somewhere to take exercise that wasn't going to expose them to the sun. There's also a laburnum arch about 30 metres (100 feet) long, which again people used to walk and talk in. The other areas of the Queen's Garden are a bit looser: there are vegetable gardens, and a lot of aromatic plants that would have been used in Georgian times for nosegays. Sanitation wasn't too good back then, and people didn't wash much, so it was important to carry around a little bunch of sweet-smelling plants that you could just stuff in your face if you met someone really ill-smelling.

The decorative features around the Queen's Garden reflect the type of things that were fashionable in the seventeenth century. We're growing apple trees in tubs, and training them to be pyramidal in shape, with short branches at the top and longer branches near the base, clipped into a neat silhouette. There's a lot of statuary, and a fountain with a figure of a boy and a dolphin in the centre.

Because the Queen's Garden is so formal it takes a great deal of maintenance. Everything has to be clipped and trimmed – it's a never-ending job. The box hedges start shooting in April and you have to keep clipping them right through till September. We've just finished pruning the hornbeam walkway, which was a huge job. We had to get scaffolding up on either side, climb up with a petrol trimmer and attack the hornbeams, then finish them off by hand. We really went for it and it looks great. Hornbeams are pretty hardy trees – they're used as street trees, so they can take a bit of rough usage. We also have a lot of yew hedges in the Queen's Garden, and they have to be clipped as well. Those formal plantations look great if they're properly maintained, but awful if you allow them to get tatty. Weeds are another problem; you just can't have weeds in a formal plantation. Sometimes I really envy the guys who work in the Natural Areas, because they actually encourage wild things to grow there, whereas we're always battling against nature in a sense.

The laburnum arch takes a good deal of maintenance, because again that's a very artificial form of planting. All the plants are intricately plaited to form the shape, so come November you have to tie in all the good strong branches and weave them across into an arch, then cut out anything that's straggly or that's growing too high. The essence of the laburnum arch is that the flowers dangle down low, so we have to keep it in shape every year. It's a long, hard job, but it's really worth it when you see the arch in full flower in April and May. It's something that people come to Kew especially to see.

Most of my work is done outdoors, I'm glad to say. When I'm not working in the Queen's Garden I'm out lending a hand with the big planting projects, like the Palm House front, or I'm taking care of management business and training. When I first applied to work at Kew back in the 1980s I was worried about being in the open air all the time; I started in winter, when it was really cold, and I wasn't sure if I could stand it. But now I wouldn't have it any other way. I must have toughened up, I suppose, because now I spend most of my time in shorts and a T-shirt, even if it's quite cold. The only time we have to go indoors is when it's raining, but even then there's no skiving off. We collect all our own seed, so one of the big indoor jobs is cleaning that up and packaging it. I look after our nurseries, which are off-limits to the public, where we propagate our bedding for future plantings, and there's always plenty to do in there, believe me.

One of the things that gives me the greatest satisfaction is reintroducing some of the old plants that have fallen out of fashion with gardeners. When I was working on the order beds we had bed after bed of daisies – asters and so on, which start to look very boring after a while. So I decided to replant the pine bed in the Duke's Garden, which is themed for late summer/autumn, with achilleas, hostas, kniphofias and delphiniums – quite old-fashioned plants that you don't see much at the moment. In the Queen's Garden I'm determined to bring back carnations and pinks. They used to be there years ago, and I always loved them, so I'm reintroducing them. I love it when a visitor sees something they've cherished in the past, and their face lights up. That's the best thing about a garden: it can bring back so many memories, just through the sight or smell of a particular plant.

TREE OF THE MONTH

The Lucombe oak *Quercus* × *hispanica* 'Lucombeana'

LOCATION: Southwest of the Palm House

DID YOU KNOW: The Lucombe oak is a comparative youngster: it is believed to have been planted at Kew in 1773, 11 years after the major plantings of 1762. This particular variety of oak was created by a horticulturist in Exeter, one Mr Lucombe, as a cross between two exotic species, *Quercus cerris* and *Q. suber*. For the first 78 years of its life it stood in the way of the proposed Syon Vista, which radiates off the rear doors of the Palm House; in 1851, the tree was dug up and transplanted 20 metres (66 feet) to the south.

THE FLOWERING OF THE TITAN ARUM

The titan arum is one of the most spectacular plants at Kew – once in a blue moon. For most of its life, this sleeping giant is a massive underground corm, weighing up to 70 kilograms (154 pounds) – the biggest of its kind in the plant kingdom. But once every few years the titan arum puts up a huge, faintly obscene-looking inflorescence that fully explains its scientific name: *Amorphophallus titanum*.

The titan arums spend their extended rest periods in the Jodrell Glasshouse, away from public view – but when one of them stirs into action it is brought to the Princess of Wales Conservatory, where crowds gather to watch it grow at a rate of 20 centimetres (8 inches) a day. Transporting it is no mean feat: the arums are grown in tubs containing about a ton of soil. Once the plant is in place, it's just a question of waiting until it flowers. At first a green, teardrop-shaped spathe appears from the ground and starts to rocket upwards. This gradually opens like an inverted umbrella, green and cream on the outside, and pinkish, deepening to red as the inflorescence matures, on the inside. As the spathe opens it reveals the spadix – a huge, yellowish-grey spike that can take the plant to a height of 3 metres (10 feet), with a circumference of 3 metres (10 feet).

Once the inflorescence is ready for pollination the fun begins. The spadix swells and belches out a smell that has been described as a mixture of rotting flesh and excrement, and the inside of the spathe turns bright crimson – all part of a strategy to fertilize the plant. The actual flowers, insignificant in appearance, are clustered around the base of the spadix, and the titan arum has to coax insects inside with its convincing imitation of decomposing flesh. The conservatory has a large population of cockroaches, who react like any beetle would to this unsubtle come-on and start swarming over the titan arum. This extreme sex show is necessary for the plant's survival as it can only sustain the display for 24 hours. Once it has flowered the whole edifice collapses quickly, to be replaced by a single, gigantic leaf, up to 6 metres (19 feet) tall and looking like a fair-sized tree.

The flowering of the titan arum is an increasingly common treat at Kew as new techniques in the glasshouse have improved propagation of the plants. Visitors who miss the final display, or who can't stand the smell or the cockroaches, can watch the flowering day by day on Kew's website.

OPPOSITE: *The flowering of the Amorphophallus titanum is an exciting event. Its smell is repellent to humans but very attractive to cockroaches.*

JULY

The heat is building, yet even in the hottest summer, Kew provides relief and shade for weary visitors who flock to this urban oasis for coolness and peace. There are shady walks by day, and music by night as the Temperate House gives itself over to the Summer Swing Festival. Tame broods of mallard and moorhen dabble on the ponds, and on warm evenings you'll hear the swifts screaming in the late, light sky as they pursue insects. And if you're lucky, you might see a flash of vivid blue around the lake, as a kingfisher carries a fish back to its perch.

This month at Kew, don't miss

- Giant waterlilies flowering in the Waterlily House and the Princess of Wales Conservatory
- Waterlilies also flowering in the Aquatic Garden
- The summer bedding in front of the Palm House
- The Duke's Garden, the Queen's Garden, the Grass Garden and the Rose Garden
- Wild flowers in Westwood Valley, Wakehurst Place

OPPOSITE: During Kew's annual Summer Swing Festival in July, spectacular fireworks light up the sky every night at ten o'clock.

GIANT WATERLILIES

There are two species of giant waterlily or *Victoria* and they can both be found growing at Kew during the summer months. *Victoria cruziana* is the smaller of the two and is grown in the Waterlily House next door to the Palm House; the larger *Victoria amazonica* is grown in the Princess of Wales Conservatory. They're both spectacular plants with enormous leaves and huge flowers – and each year, there's a race to see which one will flower first.

Named in honour of Queen Victoria, giant waterlilies are native to the huge tropical river systems of South America, where they have adapted to cope with the massive fluctuations in water levels. In cultivation, without the ability to raise or lower water levels, victorias tend to be grown as annuals, with a new plant being raised from seed each year. This is the case at Kew where, each February, dozens of *Victoria* seeds about the size of a pea are removed from their refrigerated storage and sown in one of the heated aquatic tanks in the nurseries. By mid-April, the young victorias have grown sufficiently for a single plant to be selected for planting out on public display in a huge container in their respective pools. Here, with ideal conditions and the room to grow, they really take off.

It's at this point that the rivalry between the conservatory's *V. amazonica* and the Waterlily House's *V. cruziana* kicks in. Throughout May and June the plants grow at an incredible rate, producing a new leaf every two to three days, each one bigger than the last. They reach their maximum size around midsummer, when a *V. amazonica* leaf can measure up to 2.5 metres (8 feet) across. Kew's record is 2.6 metres (8½ feet) for a leaf of a *V.* 'Longwood Hybrid', a cross between *V. cruziana* and *V. amazonica*, which was recorded in *The Guinness Book of Records*.

The new leaves emerge from the central crown or growing point like scrunched-up balls of paper. The plant pumps water through the vascular structure of these young compressed leaves, and within two to three days the leaves have inflated to their full size, just like a dinghy. The leaves will not expand any futher – so it's easy to see who's winning in the race of the giant waterlilies.

But the real prize comes not with leaf size, but with the first flowers in early July. The giant waterlily has developed an extraordinary breeding strategy. The flowers open at night in order to attract their natural pollinator, a species of night-

flying beetle. Each plant produces only one flower at a time, which lasts for just two nights. This doesn't sound like much – but the flower is the size of a dinner plate. The first night the flower opens, the petals are pure white and emit a pineapple-like scent to tempt the beetle pollinators into the flower. At this stage only the female part of the flower, the stigma, is receptive; the male parts, the anthers, have yet to release their pollen. The beetles fly into the flower and begin feeding on the nectar inside. In doing so, they brush past the stigma, transferring any pollen they may already be carrying on their bodies and thus pollinating the flower.

ABOVE: A spectacular sight awaits visitors in Kew's Waterlily House in July. The Victoria cruziana *grows rapidly over the summer months, producing a new leaf every two to three days.*

This, however, is only half the story. The *Victoria* also needs to transfer its own pollen to the flower of a different plant. So, as dawn approaches, the flower gradually closes, trapping its pollinators inside. The flower remains closed throughout the following day, during which time the anthers split, releasing pollen and dusting it over the trapped beetles. By the time the flower opens for the second night, the petals have changed colour, flushing from white to a deep pink, and are no longer visually attractive to beetles. The trapped beetles, having fed on nectar and pollen all day, are now free to go. Dusted in pollen they fly off in search of another white *Victoria* flower to feed on and pollinate. The flower gradually closes for the last time and sinks below the surface of the pond, which is when the seeds begin to develop.

If necessary, the *Victoria* will self-pollinate. At Kew, however, the glasshouse staff can act as beetle pollinators, waiting until the *Victoria* is fully opened, late at night, and then dusting pollen inside the flower using a paintbrush, thus ensuring a continued supply of seed for future generations of *Victoria* plants.

PLANT OF THE MONTH

Dragon arum *Dracunculus vulgaris*

WHERE TO SEE THEM: Woodland Garden, Kew

DID YOU KNOW: The dragon arum is a close relative of the giant titan arum that flowers in the Princess of Wales Conservatory. This species of arum, however, can be grown outdoors in pots or beds – wherever there's room for its big fat tuber. In flower, it's a stunning sight: the spathe emerges from the tuber in late spring and grows to over 60 centimetres (2 feet) high, with spectacular, stinking flowers in July. The huge erect spike in the centre of the flowers has earned the dragon arum a new common name: the Viagra lily.

MAINTAINING THE PALM HOUSE

I t was purely by chance that I made my career in horticulture. Originally I started training to be a teacher, but I wasn't happy, so I moved to Pershore College of Horticulture in Worcestershire to study for a National Diploma in Horticulture. I had a fantastic placement year working at the Cambridge University Botanic Garden as a 'trainee technician' and in my final year at Pershore I was involved with the creation of a garden for the Chelsea Flower Show. It won the coveted RHS Gold Medal and became the first gold-winning Chelsea garden that Pershore had ever built – a valuable experience that remains a treasured memory. After a further year at Pershore gaining an HND in Landscape and Amenity Management, I obtained a place on the prestigious three-year Kew Diploma Course.

Once at Kew my passion for tropical plants grew. My work placements included six months in the Palm House and over a year in total working in the Princess of Wales Conservatory. It was there that I was first given the opportunity to work with the giant waterlily. As luck would have it, the position of team leader for the Palm House and Waterlily House was advertised just months before I was due to graduate in 1999. I applied and was successful – I still feel lucky to this day.

EMMA FOX
Team Leader for the Palm House and Waterlily House

Built between 1844 and 1848, the Grade-I listed Palm House is one of the oldest surviving curvilinear glasshouses in the world. As probably the most famous building at Kew, an enormous number of visitors pass through its doors each year. Yet there's just a small team maintaining the diverse collection of tropical plants from around the world – Wesley Shaw and I are the only permanent members of staff, and we are joined by a Kew student and a trainee gardener on three-month work placements.

The Palm House plants are all grown in beds 1.7 metres (5½ feet) deep, laid out phytogeographically. That is to say, it's divided up according to where the plants originate from in the world – the north end is Australasia, the centre is the Americas and the south end is Africa. The two apse

ABOVE: Emma Fox's team have to look after the 160-year-old Palm House as well as the plants it contains. Keeping the paths and glass structure clear of algae is a full-time job.

ends of the house have been retained as a tribute to how the Victorian Palm House plants were originally grown and displayed. Here a collection of palms and cycads are grown in roll-top terracotta pots or teak boxes, which stand on the perforated cast-iron gratings that once covered the entire floor of the Palm House to allow the heat to rise through the building. The largest teak box is home to one of the oldest pot plants in the world – *Encephalartos altensteinii*, a cycad brought to Kew in 1775 by the famous plant collector Francis Masson.

The three geographic areas within the Palm House require slightly different environmental conditions. This is achieved, in part, via the climate control computer housed in my office below ground, in the bowels of the building, which controls the huge mechanical infrastructure. Fortunately for me, all I have to do is input the required temperature and humidity levels and the computer does the rest. The Palm House is kept at a minimum day temperature of 21°C (70°F), although it becomes much hotter on sunny days. Water is heated by four gas-fired boilers and is then pumped through the circuitry of pipe-work and radiators to warm the air inside the glasshouse. Located in each geographic area are sensors, which read the air temperature, feeding data back to the climate control computer every two minutes. The temperature of the hot water pipes is regulated by a system of valves, which the computer can open or close depending on the desired temperature. The climate control computer also monitors the humidity. Sensors known as hygrometers measure the relative humidity (RH) of the atmosphere inside the Palm House; if the RH falls below the desired 80%, the computer operates the misting system, and the nozzles mounted high up in the canopy release a mist of pressurized water and air, not steam as many visitors believe.

One environmental factor not controlled by the computer is the watering. Rain water is collected from the roof of the Palm House and stored in two huge underground tanks, which can hold up to 227,300 litres (50,000 gallons). We water by hand every day, using hosepipes. During the week, with four staff, the watering is usually finished before the public can enter the gardens at half past nine, but at weekends, with only one member of staff, it can take all day. Visitors really seem to enjoy watching us watering and ask all sorts of questions about how often it has to be done and whether the water has to be treated in any way. We do have a bed irrigation system installed, but we only use this on hot days to give additional water and in emergencies. I much prefer watering by hand as this gives us an opportunity to regulate the amount of water getting to a plant, as well as observe changes in plant health and condition. We don't just water the soil; we also have to spray over the canopy, increasing the humidity around the leaves and helping to wash off any plant pests.

The horticultural work in the Palm House can be quite diverse. The winter period is always busy, as this is when we prune most of the plants. Pruning lets more light through to the smaller plants, tames the faster-growing plants, which could grow through the glass and damage the building, and also allows us to remove many of the small pests that have accumulated in large numbers during the summer and autumn. We use a hydraulic platform – the 'Nifty Lift' – to access the taller trees, and this also helps us to spot the smaller pests that are difficult to see from the ground. Throughout the year we try to control the glasshouse pests using a programme of biological control. We regularly monitor the plants for initial signs of the pest and then apply specific beneficial insects to control it. These arrive at Kew by post each week, stored in special vials or tubes. We release them by sprinkling them over plants with a pest problem and leave the rest to nature.

TREE OF THE MONTH

Corsican Pine *Pinus nigra*

LOCATION: Near the Main Gate

DID YOU KNOW: This is Kew's unluckiest tree. The first 100 years of its life were uneventful enough – it was brought to Kew from the south of France in 1814 by a botanist, R. A. Salisbury, and planted in its current location a couple of years later. Disaster struck, however, in the early 1900s when a light aircraft hit the top of the tree and took out its upper branches. (The aircraft came off better, and landed safely on a nearby lawn.) Since then, the Corsican pine has been hit by lightning at least twice, the last time in 1992. There was no major damage on that occasion – some of the bark was blasted off one side of the trunk, and scarring is still visible. But lightning can be very dangerous for trees. Even a minor hit will stress them but the charge is usually carried to earth between the bark and wood, bypassing the main growing structures. An unlucky strike, however, can go right through the main trunk and blow a tree to pieces – so, to avoid that, the Corsican pine was fitted with its own lightning conductor.

An aerial-like structure was placed in the top of the tree in July 2003, with a copper conduit attached all the way down the trunk. Special sprung bolts were used for this, and allow the lightning conductor to move as the pine grows rather than becoming buried in the bark and posing a risk to the tree. A fuse fitted to the apparatus will show whether the tree has been struck by lightning during any future storms. If this lightning conductor proves to be a success in Kew's unluckiest tree, others will be fitted to taller trees around the gardens in the next few years.

Another regular job for the team is the dreaded pressure washing! The constant heat and high humidity required in the Palm House are ideal conditions for algae. Left unchecked, it will grow on the stone paths making them slippery, and also on the glass, reducing the light levels reaching the plants. Cleaning that is a bit like painting the Forth Bridge, because no sooner have you got to the end than you need to start at the beginning again. Fortunately the steady stream of students and trainees don't object, initially at least, to the task of pressure washing! Being responsible for the upkeep of the building is a huge job. There are always things going wrong – like any building made of metal and glass, the Palm House needs constant repair. If you add water to that equation, then you get an idea of the problems. The metal rusts, and the glass gets dirty. Doors are the bane of my life. The hinges are always seizing up, and it's up to me to identify and report any faults. I have to call out the buildings and maintenance team several times a week.

By late January we have usually finished pruning in the Palm House, so we turn our attentions to the Waterlily House. During the winter it's empty and closed to the public, but in early February we begin to prepare the house for the spring and summer displays. We start by replacing the soil in the beds, then planting out young plants from the nursery, which are raised from cuttings each year. We then refill the pond and allow the water to warm up to the 27°C (81°F) required for growing the tropical waterlilies that are planted out on display. When the house first opens to the public in February/March, the plants all look very small and the waterlilies have not begun to flower, but it only takes a couple of months before the house is transformed into a riot of vegetation and colour. In my opinion, the Waterlily House is at its best during June and July, as this is when the giant waterlily looks specatacular and the tropical vines are flowering and beginning to fruit. By September we have to start thinking about moving the tropical waterlilies back to their winter home in the nursery. Then the pool has to be drained and pressure-washed, ready for the purpose-built staging used for our autumn festival display of over 3000 pumpkins, squashes and gourds. This idea originated when I first began my current job, as a way of extending the season of use for the Waterlily House, and it's now become an annual event, to

which people travel from all over the country. The display takes an enormous amount of time to prepare and construct, but the finished result and the reaction of the visitors is always worth the blood, sweat and tears that went into creating it. The Waterlily House closes to the public at the end of the three-week festival and the display is dismantled. The pumpkins and squash are sold to visitors and staff, the plants and soil inside the house are removed and the whole building is pressure-washed before being 'put to bed' for the winter.

I think I have one of the best jobs at Kew – it's varied, busy and still involves the practical pleasures of horticulture. I'm very proud of what we've got here, and I really believe that the Palm House is a magical place. Even at the end of a hard day when nothing's gone right, you can look back through the Palm House, surrounded by beautiful tropical plants and suddenly everything is OK again. I love it first thing in the morning when there's nobody around; it's so quiet, it's like a cathedral. And I love it when we put the misters on full blast to damp everything down; you get shafts of low sunlight coming in through the glass, and that looks spectacular. The only downside to working in a warm wet environment is that you get a lot of colds – especially in the winter, when you have to keep nipping outside into the cold air, then coming back in here. You have to be pretty fit to work in the Palm House, because it can get very hot and humid, particularly up in the canopy. But I'll say one thing for it: it's great for keeping your weight down!

ABOVE: The Palm House's hot, humid conditions make it the perfect home for Kew's vast collection of plants from Australasia, the Americas and Africa.

OVERLEAF: The Summer Swing Jazz Festival is one of the most popular events in Kew's calendar.

113

RHODODENDRONS

The rhododendron dell at Kew has always been one of its biggest draws – and, despite the fact that rhododendrons are now recognized as an invasive foreign species inimical to native biodiversity, they still put on a terrific show. The ones at Kew and Wakehurst Place are at their peak in May, but it's during the summer months that they take up the energies of the garden staff.

Rhododendrons benefit greatly from regular pruning and deadheading. The latter also discourages the production of seeds, which can be stored in the soil in such quantities as to crowd out all other plant life. The flower heads are easy to remove. After they've bloomed, and the seeds have started to ripen, the stem forms a natural break with the main plant and this can be broken with a simple twist. But there are thousands upon thousands of flower heads to be tackled, and not enough staff to go round – which means roping in volunteers to help complete the huge task.

It takes 16 people (eight arboretum staff and eight volunteers) up to two weeks to deadhead all the rhododendrons in the dell at Kew – an awful lot of man-hours. The flower heads are collected in buckets, then put into trailers and taken straight back to the Stable Yard where they're shredded and added to the compost heaps. Like everything else at Kew, they go straight back into the natural cycle.

OPPOSITE: The Rhododendron Dell in full flower is a stunning sight.

AUGUST

Summer is drawing to its close, the flowers start to give way to fruits, and the nights are gradually falling earlier. The gardens are still beautiful, with a final flush of summer bedding and bushes, the hydrangeas and hibiscus at their blowsy best. And in the woodlands, the brambles are laden with blackberries, providing an enormous feast for every bird and beast with a taste for fresh fruit.

This month at Kew, don't miss

- Summer bulbs and scented plants near King William's Temple
- Hibiscus, hydrangeas and Indian bean trees throughout the gardens
- Spectacular summer bedding in the Order Beds and in the Pleasaunce, Wakehurst Place
- Mixed herbaceous plantings in the Water Garden, Wakehurst Place
- Mixed cottage plantings in the Sir Henry Price Garden, Wakehurst Place
- *Hedychium* in the Monocotyledon Border, Wakehurst Place
- *Eucryphia* in the Southern Hemisphere Garden, Wakehurst Place

OPPOSITE: The beautiful mansion at Wakehurst Place seen from across the waterlily pond – the perfect setting for a tranquil summer afternoon.

WORKING WITH THE CLIMATE

Climate change is an increasingly important factor at Kew. The south of England is becoming warmer and drier – and this means plants that enjoy a lot of water are starting to struggle, despite the best efforts of staff to keep them well irrigated.

In terms of drought 2003 was a particularly bad year. A dry spring was followed by a long, hot summer and a dry autumn, which meant that trees, in particular, started to feel the pinch. By July, the arboretum team noticed that many of them were going into what they call 'September mode' – shutting down, withdrawing nutrients into their main bodies, budding up and losing leaf, just as they would in autumn. It's a normal survival strategy for dry weather – if you see a tree shedding its leaves early, it probably means it will ride out the drought because it's responding to the adverse conditions and fighting back. If the leaves drop, they'll come again; more worrying is when leaves go dry and brown but stay on a tree. This means that the natural processes have been interrupted, and it is on the way out. Beeches are particularly vulnerable to drought, as are birches, cherries and some of the pines. They prefer to keep their feet wet, and the combination of Kew's sandy soil and a protracted lack of rain can prove fatal.

Dry weather in itself won't kill trees; the real problems begin when latent threats, like honey fungus and other diseases, start to get a grip on specimens already weakened by lack of water. The effects of drought aren't always apparent at first, and it can be two or three years before it is possible to assess the scale of any damage. Some trees come back after a dry year and look pretty healthy, but in fact they're dying inside. They've used too many of their internal resources, which can only be depleted to a certain level before trees lose the ability to replenish themselves. And so, over a few years, they become weaker and more vulnerable, waiting only for some secondary problem to come along and finish them off.

The period from April to October is usually the arboretum team's maintenance period – this is when they must prune the trees and keep them tidy and weed-free. But the 2003 drought disrupted the usual routine, and obliged everyone to turn their hand to irrigation. For six weeks during the summer the entire team

OPPOSITE: During a very dry summer, the arboretum team spend most of their time keeping Kew's trees watered. Young trees often suffer the worst in a drought, as their roots aren't long enough to reach down to natural water sources.

was on watering duties every single day, with no time for cleaning up, let alone carrying out more routine maintenance work – and this was just to keep the trees alive through the worst of the heatwave. The knock-on effect, of course, was that much of the maintenance work didn't get done, and this can have a further impact on trees already stressed by lack of water. Even with a team of 20 staff working flat out, it was impossible to get to all the ones that needed irrigation on a regular basis.

Trees at Kew aren't usually watered very often. When they're small they need additional moisture in order to get a root system established, but once they've developed into young trees they should be able to get enough water through the natural provision of rain, mist and dew. In fact, it's not good practice to water trees too frequently, as this keeps the roots too near the surface, where there's easy water, and prevents them digging down to deeper, more reliable sources. If a young tree is overwatered it becomes entirely dependent on the gardener – and the moment the watering stops, it will die. The most vulnerable trees in a garden are youngsters: trees that are no longer in baskets, but which don't yet have substantial deep roots that will reach down to water.

Nature operates on a system of checks and balances, so even a drought of the severity of the one in 2003 isn't entirely bad news for Kew. Like storms, long periods of dry weather bring about a natural culling of trees, killing off weaker specimens and making way for new plants. This works in botanical gardens as well as in the wild – and, in the case of Kew where space is very limited, it can open up new areas for planting, thereby increasing the scientific collection and contributing to genetic diversity among the plants. And there's another advantage to dry weather: weeds don't flourish.

A drought impacts on different parts of Kew in different ways. For lawns it's a disaster, as anyone who tried to keep their grass green through the summer of 2003 knows. Bedding plants, with their shallow roots, need constant watering. But in the natural areas of Kew a drought isn't a problem. Trees will die, but this means there's more dead wood to feed insects and create habitats for plants and fungi. If bark drops off and holes form in tree trunks, there are suddenly a lot of

PLANT OF THE MONTH

Hardy banana *Ensete ventricosum*

WHERE TO SEE IT: Exotic border next to
Cambridge Cottage

DID YOU KNOW: Not the great big edible variety of
banana, this is nonetheless a splendid ornamental
plant that produces spectacular foliage in the summer
months. The hardy banana is at its biggest and best in
August – and at Kew it has even been known to bear
flowers. These can turn into small green fruit, but
won't develop or ripen.

desirable residences in the woodland for bats. A drought means that meadows dry
out quickly – and the plants that bloom in them go into survival overdrive,
flowering like crazy in order to make more seed for what they hope will be a
wetter season the following year. Fruits are produced for longer and ripen earlier,
providing an abundance of food for animals. And a long, dry summer can lead
to a spectacular display of colour before the leaves drop.

But what does climate change mean for the future of the arboretum? It has
been battling with the effects of drought since the mid 1970s – and the change
in the weather, combined with Kew's thin, sandy soil, means it's no longer
possible to grow trees that need a lot of water. The solution to the problem is
to reposition the collection with introductions from drier parts of the world.
Some parts of China, the Mediterranean and North America are rich in dry,
warm habitats – and trees from these regions are doing very well indeed in the
gardens. The loss of established specimens through drought is sad, but their
failure gives an opportunity to other ones that are better suited to the conditions.
As with all things at Kew, it's a question of long-term planning.

EXPANDING THE COLLECTION

I have one of the most far-reaching jobs at Kew. A couple of years ago the arboretum and horticultural services were amalgamated, so not only do I look after all the trees and shrubs in the arboretum, but I'm also responsible for all the machinery like mowers and chainsaws, all the grass cutting and the green-waste recycling.

Taking care of the arboretum doesn't just mean supervising the day-to-day management of over 14,000 trees. It also involves curating the collection, making sure we have a good representation of a wide variety of different trees and shrubs. To that end, I'm responsible for collecting plants for Kew – and that means going on field trips. My first trip for Kew was to Chile in 1985; since then I've been to South Korea, Taiwan, the Russian Far East, Japan and China, where I've been four times. I've concentrated on the temperate Far East because that's an area in which we needed to strengthen our collection at Kew.

TONY KIRKHAM
Head of the
Arboretum and
Horticultural Services

There's a great sense of urgency about getting into China because plants and habitats are disappearing very fast there. China is changing at an alarming rate due to agricultural clearance and mass felling for timber production. It's slowing down a bit now; there's been a blanket ban on felling in 12 provinces, not for conservation reasons but because they were experiencing massive flooding of the Yangtze basin. There were no trees to soak up the water as it ran off the mountains, and so it was rushing down with loads of silt and flooding the central plain. Things are slightly better now, and there are many national parks and conservation areas springing up, but the loss of habitat is still appalling.

We were recently in Sichuan province and brought back 159 seed collections. It's an area we've concentrated on because plants from there do very well in Kew; they're suited to our climate. Other provinces are a lot wetter, and plants from these won't flourish in the relatively dry, warm conditions we have. Sichuan is also reasonably accessible, and we didn't want to go anywhere that would pose enormous administrative problems or duplicate the work of other botanic gardens.

Sichuan is very rich in vegetation, and so I was able to draw up a big target list of things we were looking for. It was several pages long and contained maples, birches, horse chestnuts, *Cotoneaster*, *Berberis* and loads of rhododendrons – things that sound like familiar garden plants, but there are many species within each group and we don't have all of them here. When I was drawing up the target list I consulted the field notes of Ernest Wilson, a celebrated plant collector who went to the same area in Sichuan in 1910 and brought back an enormous number of plants – almost everyone who has a garden in Britain has a Wilson plant in it. I got his field notes from the Herbarium and archives, looked at what he'd found back then and tried to find as many of those plants as possible. I looked at his photographs and studied his journals, because I wanted to follow in his footsteps. Wilson kept accurate records, and so we could tell we were in exactly the same spot where he had stood. If a plant is no longer growing there, you can be pretty sure it's been lost to that region.

We flew to Chengdu, then did a big circuit north and northwest of there – a total of 4000 kilometres (2490 miles) in four weeks. We were on the move pretty much all the time. Occasionally we stayed for a couple of days in the same place, but normally we were travelling every day. Sometimes, in the more remote areas, we camped out – and to be honest I prefer that, because your tent's your own and it's clean inside as long as you keep it that way. The hotels, on the other hand…well, let's just say that you tend to sleep in your sleeping bag rather than in the bed. And then there's the nightlife – the rats running above your head, the snakes, the cockroaches. The rats are the worst; I can't stand hearing them scampering across the floor above me. I just put on my Walkman and go to sleep listening to music. They're a real nuisance when they come into the room, because they'll eat your seed collection if you're not careful.

The trip went incredibly well. The weather was lovely and there was no rain for the whole four weeks, which is unheard of in western China. When it rains, it really rains: the rivers regularly flood, there are landslides and roads get washed away, so it can be very difficult to get around. But we were lucky this time – and I didn't get sick either, which is very rare because you usually get diarrhoea. You have to be very careful about what you drink or brush your teeth with in China. These are remote rural areas, and the water supply isn't very safe. I've had bad experiences before; the first time I ever went on a field trip for Kew, to Chile in 1985, I got salmonella and was very sick for five days. That trip was a bit of a washout!

What we're looking for on a collecting trip are seeds. We don't bring back any living material, except the occasional cutting of a willow or poplar – we're certainly not digging up trees and shipping them home. So we need to find fertile trees, then we'll collect the seeds and take a 'voucher' – a sample that comes back to the Herbarium at Kew and gets the same collection number as the seeds we collect. That number stays with the plant right from germination, all through its life in the garden, and the voucher enables the botanists to identify it.

When we're out in the field we try to clean up the seeds, taking off any of the fruit, drying the seeds and packaging them. Then they come back to Kew where they go straight into quarantine to make sure they've got no bugs or diseases, after which they go to the nursery to be propagated. It takes about two years before we've got a plant that's ready for the garden. From every seed collection, I aim to get about ten living plants. I might only want one or two for Kew, so I pick the best specimen; the rest of them are given to other botanic gardens or institutions.

On the trip to China I tried to be very focused on what I really needed for Kew. It would have been easy to bring back 300 or 400 collections, but I wouldn't have had anywhere to put them. There's a limit to the weight of seed you're allowed to bring out of China, so I didn't want to waste that on a dozen unnamed *Cotoneaster* or *Philadelphus* that I had no real need for. As it is, I know exactly where everything is going. I'm planning to replant the rhododendron dell over the next three to five years – we're going to create something that's much more like a Chinese gorge, with different layers of vegetation rather than just the rhodos. It's important to re-create those habitats because it's a way of getting the conservation message across to our visitors.

That's something we're concentrating on much more these days – creating habitats that have an educational value. In the redwood grove, for instance, we've planted a greater number of trees, and we've killed off the grass that used to grow under them because it created a very sterile environment; it now resembles a forest floor and when you go in there you really could be in California. And in the Mediterranean planting around King William's Temple we're putting in olive trees and cork oaks, to tell a story about the social and economic importance of those plants. Every planting should tell a story, rather than just being a systematic group of plants. In the past we had beds and beds of cotoneasters, for instance, which nobody looked at, not even the scientists. If the scientists aren't looking at them, you certainly can't expect the visitors to learn anything!

One of the major things we gain from field trips, quite apart from the acquisition of plants, is a greater understanding of how things behave in the wild. I always keep a diary in which I record how different species grow together,

ABOVE: Kew aims to preserve plants that grow in threatened habitats around the world by collecting seed and bringing it back to Kew. Rhododendrons, such as this one in China, are then grown at Kew, where they thrive in the sandy soil.

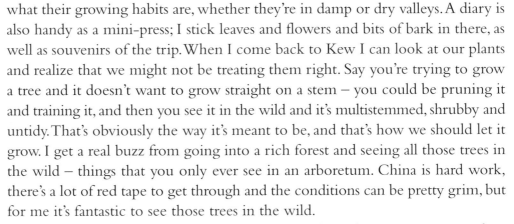

what their growing habits are, whether they're in damp or dry valleys. A diary is also handy as a mini-press; I stick leaves and flowers and bits of bark in there, as well as souvenirs of the trip. When I come back to Kew I can look at our plants and realize that we might not be treating them right. Say you're trying to grow a tree and it doesn't want to grow straight on a stem – you could be pruning it and training it, and then you see it in the wild and it's multistemmed, shrubby and untidy. That's obviously the way it's meant to be, and that's how we should let it grow. I get a real buzz from going into a rich forest and seeing all those trees in the wild – things that you only ever see in an arboretum. China is hard work, there's a lot of red tape to get through and the conditions can be pretty grim, but for me it's fantastic to see those trees in the wild.

I'm what we call a 'lifer' here at Kew. I've been here since 1978, when I started on the Kew Diploma Course. When they gave me my first job, as a manager of the arboretum at the north end of the gardens, I thought I'd give it three years and then move on. Twenty-five years later I'm still here, and I'll never move. You either love Kew or loathe it. It doesn't suit everyone, and those people leave after two years. But those of us who stay are really dedicated; we love what we do, we're passionate about plants and we have the opportunity to pioneer new horticultural techniques. Kew doesn't have a great deal of money, so we have to work with partners who can help with funding – but we do have the name, the clout, that enables us to do things like get permits from Beijing for a Chinese expedition. There aren't many places in the world that could do that.

I try to get outdoors in the gardens as much as I can, although there's a lot of office work as well. Most of the staff finish work at quarter past three, so if I have serious paperwork to do I start it then because I know I won't be disturbed. I have to go to a lot of meetings – seeing reps about products and machinery, attending management meetings about budgets, health and safety and forward planning. But wherever possible, I like to walk the job. I love to look at the trees in the arboretum. I dress in a polo-shirt and jeans most of the time. I never know when I'm going to have to get underneath a piece of machinery to sort out a problem, and I don't think a suit and tie would be appropriate for that!

TREE OF THE MONTH

Turner's oak *Quercus* × *turneri*

LOCATION: Near the Princess of Wales Conservatory

DID YOU KNOW: Mr Turner, an Essex botanist, created this hybrid by crossing *Quercus robur* and *Q. ilex* in the late eighteenth century, and this specimen was soon introduced to Kew as part of the 2-hectare (5-acre) arboretum in 1798. Like many trees of its age, it was beginning to look a little tired towards the end of the twentieth century, and when the great storm of 1987 struck it seemed a certain candidate for destruction.

What happened during that storm, however, was beneficial to the old Turner's oak, and eventually to many other trees in the gardens. The winds got underneath its canopy and actually lifted the tree slightly out of the ground. Then, miraculously, it settled back in again and remained securely anchored in the soil. After its little airing the Turner's oak seemed to spring back to life, and it soon became apparent that the disturbance of the soil had been extremely good for it. Generations of visitors had taken shelter under the tree's enormous canopy during showers – and this had led to the soil becoming seriously compacted, making it difficult for water and nutrients to get down to the oak's roots. So successful was the accidental decompaction that it was one of the factors that led to a systematic programme of soil decompaction for older trees all over Kew.

CONING OF THE CYCADS

Two ancient Mexican cycads, a male and a female, have lived on either side of a path in the Palm House since 1888 without managing to produce an heir. These prehistoric plants, which have evolved very little since they shared the Earth with the dinosaurs, don't make life easy for themselves: they cone only once in seven years, and even then it's touch and go whether or not the male and female will cone at the same time, thus enabling pollination to take place.

One of the Kew cycads, *Dioon spinulosum*, last coned in 1996, so when Wesley Shaw, higher botanical horticulturist in the Palm House, noticed that the female was producing a cone in the summer of 2003, he realized there was a chance that the plants might breed. When the female cone is ready to receive pollen it opens up its lower scales. In the wild, this would enable small beetles to crawl inside, spreading pollen collected from nearby male cones. Kew's female appeared to be ready to mate – the only problem being that her nearby husband was slow off the mark. And so began a race against time. The female will only remain receptive for a week, after which there's nothing for it but to wait another seven years.

Happily for all concerned, the male cycad began to shed its pollen on the sixth day of the week, and so his cone was cut and placed on paper. The collected pollen was mixed with water into a fertilizing goo, then sucked up into a turkey baster and injected into the top of the receptive female cone. The internal structure of this is helical – so when the pollen mixture started running out of the open scales at the bottom, Shaw knew the female flowers inside had all had a good chance of being pollinated.

After this artificial 'insemination' the team had to wait to see if fertilization had actually taken place. And, gradually, the female cone began to grow, proving that the seeds inside were expanding as they approached maturity. At full size a fertile cone weighs about 15 kilograms (33 pounds) after growing at a rate of 2 centimetres (¾ inch) a week. The maturing process can take anything up to a year, but when the cone is ready it splits open to release the seeds into the ground. The next step is to collect them and test them for fertility. They are put in a bucket of water and as the fertile seeds are heavier they sink to the bottom – a rather crude method, but it works.

Cycads can produce up to 300 plants per cone, so even a 10 per cent germination rate could create 30 new specimens of a species that's seriously endangered in the wild.

Summer 2003 was the first time the Palm House cycads had ever coned together. Usually the pollen is collected and then refrigerated until the female cones – but it goes off very quickly, and previously the botanists had never achieved a successful pollination. This time it all came together, and they are hopeful that Kew has made a major contribution to the survival of the plant.

ABOVE: Wesley Shaw checks the cycads in the Palm House for signs of pollen, before the first ever successful coning of the plants in 2003.

SEPTEMBER

Summer is turning into autumn in the gardens. The first of the colour appears in the trees, the overture to the great climax of the botanical year, as Kew changes from green to gold. In the woodland areas fungi are popping up in the leaf litter, while the first of the berries are appearing on the fruiting bushes. Look down the grassy rides of Queen Charlotte's Gardens and see green woodpeckers burying acorns in the turf, a handy store against a hard winter. And as one cycle ends, another begins: students are coming in to the School of Horticulture, starting the year with the traditional clog and apron race.

This month at Kew, don't miss

- Bulbs in the Woodland Glade
- Hardy cyclamen throughout the gardens
- Kew's first glorious burst of autumn colour
- *Polygonum affine* in the Slips, Wakehurst Place
- *Polygonum vacciniifolium* in the Himalayan Glade, Wakehurst Place

OPPOSITE: *An aerial view of the Pagoda Vista looking towards the Palm House gives a glimpse of just a small part of Kew's extensive arboretum.*

MAKING MULCH

Anyone who visits Kew in early autumn has to watch out for trucks and trailers rolling along the paths of the arboretum. September is the time for mulching, and it's then that the year-round programme of recycling reaps rewards.

About 98 per cent of Kew's green waste is recycled – that's everything that comes from the gardens, with a few notable exceptions. Persistent, invasive weeds like ground elder, bindweed and *Oxalis* are bagged up and destroyed – no amount of chopping up or rotting down will stop these great survivors from spreading. Anything that's obviously diseased, like the roots of a tree infected with honey fungus, is also removed from the gardens. But everything else – weeds, tree brush, grass cuttings, you name it – is brought back to the Stable Yard where it's added to the enormous, steaming compost heaps that dominate this part of the gardens. Visitors can see the splendour of these from a specially constructed viewing platform near the yard.

Creating compost at Kew is similar to making it in private gardens, but on a grand scale. All the waste that comes into the Stable Yard is put through shredding machines that chop it up into bite-sized pieces – a process that greatly accelerates the rotting process. These are then graded into different sizes according to the heap they will go on. Kew produces different mulch 'recipes' for different purposes. A woody one is useful for top-dressing a young tree, keeping the moisture in and the weeds down, and releasing its nutrients over a long, slow period; a finer mulch, made of the green parts of plants, is used for enriching and aerating soil; and a decorative one made from the smallest, softest vegetation, which rots down to create a fine, dark and attractive mulch, is perfect for putting round display plantings.

Once the garden waste has been graded and sorted to make the different recipes, it's mixed with horse manure and added to the enormous piles in the centre of the Stable Yard. Kew recycles up to 10,000 cubic metres (more than 350,000 cubic feet) of raw plant waste every year, producing plenty of usable compost for the gardens. The piles look more like ancient burial mounds than regular compost heaps.

What first catches the eye is the vapour coming off each pile. The decay of vegetable matter creates heat, which in turn accelerates the decay, and the mounds are basically smouldering away at temperatures of 60°C (140°F) or more. Temperatures are checked every day by sticking a long thermometer into the heart of every pile. Water and air spark off the bacteria that cause rotting, so it's important to keep the compost damp and well aired throughout the process.

Because of the size of Kew's heaps, the temperatures they reach and the proliferation of bacteria it doesn't take long for garden waste to rot down; in fact, most of the mounds turn raw material into usable mulch within 12 weeks. Returning to the soil is a vital part of the life cycle of all plant matter at Kew – not only does this enrich the naturally sandy soil, and cut down on weeds and watering, but it also saves the gardens hundreds of thousands of pounds every year. Waste disposal and fertilizer cost a fortune – but Kew's home-baked mulch is absolutely free.

AN EMPHASIS ON EDUCATION

OPPOSITE: Every autumn the trees in the Woodland Garden shed their leaves, creating a fiery carpet round the Temple of Aeolus.

IAN LEESE
Principal of the
School of Horticulture

I run the Kew Diploma Course, which is a three-year, full-time course, as well as an internship programme that offers three months of practical experience around the gardens.

There are only 14 places on the diploma course, so competition is pretty fierce and we have to go through a very careful selection procedure to make sure we're getting the right people. Every year we get about 300 requests for applications, out of which come around 100 actual applicants. We narrow that down to a shortlist of 30 who we interview, and then take on 14, so just under 50 per cent of the people we interview get on to the course. It's open to anyone with two years' practical experience in horticulture, some formal horticultural training and academic achievements to A level equivalent in a science subject. We have to set fairly stringent entry requirements because otherwise we'd be swamped with applications from people who aren't really serious about horticulture. Once they find out that they have to have some solid experience behind them, the casual applicants will drop out.

The most important thing for us is practical experience. Obviously there's a strong academic element to the course, but what we're really looking for is people who know how to translate that academic know-how into real garden work. The best qualification as far as we're concerned is some work experience in a botanic garden; we get a lot of people who have worked at places like Chelsea Physic Garden, the Oxford and Cambridge Botanic Gardens, and the Royal Horticultural Society's Wisley Gardens. These are all important recruiting grounds for us, and increasingly we're taking on people who have done the

internship at Kew or our own paid apprenticeship for new entrants to the industry, the Rotational Training Scheme. We've seen them, they've seen us and we're likely to have an understanding of whether they're suited.

Successful students have to have an excellent knowledge of plants and be able to demonstrate this in the interview. There's a practical assessment as well as an interview, and they have to pass a plant-identification test. We show them a whole range of trees, shrubs, bedding and house plants, and we're looking for the full Latin name, the genus and the species. There's also a plant propagation test to make sure they know their way round a nursery, and an assessment of whether they can use horticultural machinery safely. We don't actually get them to handle a hedge trimmer or a motor mower, but they have to talk us through the process.

The Kew Diploma Course is very focused, and much more work-oriented than a university course. We don't have long vacations. Basically, the students are working for three years. When I was at university I got sidetracked into things like writing for the student paper – but at Kew you have to be very dedicated to your practical work and your studies. It's a job, not a holiday. During their time here the students go through all the main parts of the garden: they work in the arboretum, in hardy display and in the greenhouses, spending a year in each. Within each area there are smaller units; within hardy display, for instance, there's bedding, herbaceous and alpine. So the students are moving every three months, getting hands-on experience of every aspect of Kew's work. There are opportunities for those who want to specialize; you can work with the tree gang, for instance, or in the micropropagation unit.

There's really nothing like the Kew Diploma Course anywhere else in the world. Wisley does a two-year course, but it doesn't have the same academic standards. Cambridge runs a two-year apprenticeship scheme in the botanic gardens, and there are courses in New York and Niagara Falls that are both modelled on the Kew course, but which don't have the same kind of international recognition. Our diploma is the equivalent of a university degree, and after graduating a lot of students go on to do a master's elsewhere. After they've worked their way round Kew, which is a centre of excellence and

expertise, our students have got the best all-round training to be had anywhere in the world. They learn everything from entomology to driving a tractor.

We have a lot of international students now, and the age range goes from 19 to over 40, so there's a great deal of diversity in the student body and they get a lot out of that as well. In addition to the on-site training, there are travel opportunities too: in 2003 we had students on scholarships to Cameroon, Ecuador, the United States and India. There's a third-year scholarship to spend a year in the botanic gardens in Jerusalem, and then there's a major travel scholarship for one student at the end of the course to go, this year, to Barbados.

I was a student on the Kew Diploma Course myself, from 1979 to 1982, and it was quite different in those days. We spent the first four months entirely in the lecture theatre preparing for exams. We led a very sheltered existence and saw hardly anything of the gardens because we were always in the school! Nowadays we start them off in September with three weeks of introductory lectures about Kew and the course, then we pack them off into the gardens for six months and don't see them in the lecture theatre again until April, by which time they've met everyone and have a much better idea of what Kew is all about.

Kew opened many doors for me. On my first day I attended a guest lecture by Roy Lancaster, a great horticulturist whom I'd seen on TV – and I was very inspired and impressed to be in the presence of this famous guy! I made friends for life here

ABOVE: While on the three-year diploma course, students spend time helping in every part of the gardens, including the Lower Nursery where supplies of cacti, orchids and ferns are grown for stock material and scientific research.

OVERLEAF: Thanks to Kew's well maintained arboretum, a visit to the gardens in the autumn promises a visual feast of colour and contrast.

and we have great reunions; Kew people are everywhere. And I had the most wonderful travel opportunities. I went to Switzerland in my second year to study alpine flora, and I won the third-year travel scholarship to Barbados and Martinique.

Kew is the greatest calling card any horticulturist could wish for, and with the added prestige of becoming a World Heritage Site we have even more clout in the international world of plants and gardens than ever before. We're trying to respond to that by putting more and more emphasis on education – not just through the school, but by making our expertise available to the world at large through the website. That's definitely the big expansion for the future. We can only take on 14 people a year for the diploma course, but we have a responsibility to disseminate our expertise as much as we possibly can.

TREE OF THE MONTH

Chinese tulip tree *Liriodendron chinense*

LOCATION: Chinese Tulip Tree Avenue

DID YOU KNOW: The Chinese species of the tulip tree is fast becoming rare in the wild because of intensive felling programmes across its native habitat. Fortunately, however, Kew has been active in preserving the species through the collection of wild seed, and the latest planting (in 2001), of 28 young trees, re-creates the old tulip tree avenue that was one of the original features of the arboretum.

The seed for the trees comes from Micang Shan in the Sichuan province of China. A batch was first collected from a specimen found in primary forest in 1996 – but it produced only a handful of young trees. Three years later, the Kew team returned to Micang Shan to collect more seed – and found their tree standing all on its own in a felling site, all its neighbours long gone. It owed its survival to the fact that it formed a handy anchor for a speedline that loggers used to move their wood from the felling site to the roadside. Because of the stress this placed on it, the tree had gone into survival overdrive, producing much more seed than it normally would in undisturbed forest.

Bad news for the tree's native habitat, then – but good news for Kew, where the mass planting of Chinese tulip trees will provide genetic diversity and should ensure the long-term preservation of a threatened species.

THE CLOG AND APRON RACE

Like any college, Kew's School of Horticulture has its fair share of history and tradition, as well as many famous alumni. The writer and broadcaster Alan Titchmarsh was a student from 1969 to 1972, and well remembers the wooden clogs with metal heels that gardeners wore for working in the glasshouses, as well as the traditional apron that was the uniform of all the gardening staff in the first half of the twentieth century. He keeps up his connections with Kew and was the guest of honour at the school's prize-giving day in 2003.

Clogs and aprons may have been discarded in favour of trainers and fleeces, but they still have an outing in the annual race that inaugurates the academic year

PLANT OF THE MONTH

Hardy cyclamen *Cyclamen hederifolium*

WHERE TO SEE THEM: Woodland Garden; Rock Garden; under clipped hedges in the Queen's Garden and Duke's Garden

DID YOU KNOW: Many bulbous plants provide a colourful complement to autumn foliage, and none does better at Kew than the hardy cyclamen. A Mediterranean plant, it thrives in dry, shady conditions. The first flowers can appear in late July, but the best show is in September, when the contrast between the mauves, whites and pinks of the cyclamen and the yellows and browns of the leaves is most striking. There are other bulbous plants in the gardens in autumn – notably colchicums and autumn-flowering species of the true crocus, like the beautiful blue *Crocus speciosa* – but the cyclamen are the most spectacular and the most reliable.

at the School of Horticulture. All the new students don the outfit and run down the Broad Walk, from the 'roundabout' flower bed at the Palm House to the Orangery, a course of 340 metres (372 yards). The record, long held by a student who won the race in 1951, was broken in 2002 by Kate Jenrick, the first woman to win and a member of a running club.

Ian Leese, the principal of the school, admits that he flunked the race when he was a freshman in 1979, his excuse being that the BBC World Service were in attendance and nobbled him for an interview. Since returning as head of the school in 1989, however, he has made up for this by running with the students every year – and always makes a point of crossing the finishing line with the slowest runner, 'so that they won't come in last by themselves'.

Another, less venerable, school tradition is 'Pranks Day', which traditionally happens in the same week that the third-year students graduate. Over the years, the school and gardens have been festooned with several miles of toilet roll, and the outgoing students have dismantled tractors and reassembled them inside the school, converted grass areas into golf courses and stuck a 'For Sale' sign outside the director's house. One summer, when the Palm House bedding consisted largely of ornamental vegetables, they placed several 'Pick Your Own' signs around the beds, much to the confusion of the visiting public.

Pranks Day, however, shows signs of dying out: in 2003 the graduating students decided not to continue the tradition, possibly to the relief of the school staff.

ABOVE: At the start of each school year, new students line up for the traditional clog and apron race – a reminder of the uniforms that gardening staff wore over 50 years ago.

OCTOBER

The autumn colour at both Kew and Wakehurst Place has to be seen to be believed. From every point in the gardens the eye is assaulted by spectacular shades of red and yellow, while the ground is carpeted with the first fall of dry, brown leaves. That's the cue for the mulching team at Kew to spring into action, busting up the leaves *in situ* for the worms to take down into the earth, feeding next year's growth. The trees may be going to sleep, but preparations are already well under way for next spring, as the staff busy themselves with the massive annual planting of bulbs throughout the gardens. Watch out for well-fed wood pigeons, squirrels and jays making the most of the abundant acorn harvest.

This month at Kew, don't miss

- The intense autumn colour at Kew and Wakehurst Place
- The Pumpkin Festival in the Waterlily House
- Autumn-flowering crocuses, colchicums and hardy cyclamen throughout the gardens

OPPOSITE: The gardens are quieter now after the busy summer months. Enhanced by autumn mists, the beauty of the buildings and the trees is evident.

PLANTING BULBS

The crocus carpet is one of the great annual delights of Kew Gardens – a huge swathe of colour, comprising over 1.6 million plants, across the lawns between Victoria Gate and King William's Temple. The display is at its best in February and March – but the hard work of creating the crocus carpet, and the many other bulb displays at Kew, is done months before, in October. This is when the arboretum team take a break from tending the larger plants and get down to ground level, digging in thousands of bulbs every year.

Bulbs need refreshing or replenishing on a regular basis and, while most of them will come back year after year, spreading and naturalizing with time, it's important to keep the displays at their best by adding fresh stock in the autumn, replacing any casualties and increasing the density and range of the plantations. In recent years, as many as 1.25 million bulbs have been planted throughout the gardens. Although it seems a lot, spread across Kew's acres it's a fairly modest amount – but enough to maintain the spring impact visitors have come to expect. As well as the main crocus carpet, which was topped up in 2002 with a further 750,000 bulbs, there are always new areas to colonize in the autumn. Around 300,000 scilla have been planted beside the Cherry Walk as well as 600,000 *Crocus tommasinianus* along paths, 110,000 *Narcissus pseudonarcissus* in long-grass areas, and a modest 250,000 *Fritillaria meleagris* in a damp area near the Palm House. The most recent addition to Kew's bulb family is the *Camassia*, a plant with a blue-flowering spike; 5000 have been planted as an experiment, and if they do well, they'll naturalize and increase in numbers.

Bulbs are a key component of Kew's strategy to provide year-round colour for visitors to the gardens; they're among the first plants to show after the winter, and they bridge a gap before the onset of flowering shrubs and bedding plants. In small-scale domestic gardens, bulb planting is a pleasant autumn job spread over a couple of afternoons at the most. In Kew, however, it's a massive task that can take up most of October. Technology is helping to reduce the time it takes, and is also saving the backs and legs of the staff.

Smaller, harder bulbs and corms, like crocus, *N. pseudonarcissus* and scilla, can be rotivated into the soil, provided they haven't started to produce vulnerable

new shoots. It's a disarmingly easy process: the turf is removed from the area, the soil is rotivated fairly deeply, the bulbs are scattered over the freshly dug earth and the rotavator is then taken over the area again, on a very slow setting, to turn the bulbs into the ground, exactly as raisins are folded into a cake mixture. It's not an instant process. It still takes a team of 12 people over a week to get 750,000 bulbs into the ground, even with a rotavator – but it's four times faster than the old, manual method, and much less dangerous in terms of back injury.

Softer bulbs, like daffodils, need gentler handling but there are still labour-saving devices to take the pain out of planting. A hollow-tine aerating machine is usually used to aerate grass areas – it takes a core out of the soil, which is then dressed with sand. It is also handy for digging a lot of holes that are just the right width and depth for the bulbs. Once any long grass has been cut down, and the soil has been irrigated so that it's soft enough for the tines to lift, the machine is run over the area a few times to create a random distribution of holes. The bulbs are dropped into the holes, a top dressing is applied and the job's done.

Sometimes, though, there's nothing for it but good, old-fashioned manual labour – for instance, where digging equipment would damage the bulbs. And wooded areas in the arboretum can't be worked on with machinery because of the network of tree roots near ground level – a rotavator would damage the trees, and a hollow-tine machine would never get through the roots. The low-tech solution: a team of gardeners with trowels, knee pads and a lot of patience.

ABOVE: Autumn is one of the busiest times of year for those who work at Kew. Every year thousands of bulbs are planted all over the gardens, in preparation for another colourful spring.

PLANT OF THE MONTH
Clerodendrum trichotomum

WHERE TO SEE IT: Museum border near Victoria Gate

DID YOU KNOW: *Clerodendrum trichotomum* var. *fargesii* is an obscure autumn star at Kew. This decorative shrub doesn't even have a common name, even though it's available through many garden suppliers and fairly widely known in British gardens. It has elegant, star-like flowers in the summer, but it's in the autumn months that it really comes into its own, with an incredible display of blue berries surrounded by red cadices.

Bulb planting is a nerve-racking job. It's impossible to know until the following spring whether it has been successful and Kew's budget for bulbs is many thousands of pounds every year. There was much trepidation after the introduction of rotavator-assisted planting – would the blades simply smash the bulbs to pieces? – but having seen how successful it is this method is now being used to extend Kew's famous spring show to parts of the gardens where bulbs have never yet been seen.

Once the bulbs are up and in bud, what happens next depends on the elements. Crocus are notoriously fragile plants and a badly timed storm can smash them to pieces before they reach full bloom. But a kind spring allows the flowers to open fully, providing up to six weeks of dazzling, unforgettable colour. The display is a magnet to visitors – and a favourite with Kew staff, many of whom can be found in silent admiration of the crocus carpet in the early mornings, when they have it all to themselves.

CREATING THE MARINE COLLECTION

I came to Kew in 1985 after seeing an advert in *New Scientist* saying that they were looking for someone to develop a collection of living marine plants. The job started with a clean slate. The curator of the day was conscious of the fact that all the skills at Kew were land-based, and he just said to me, 'We want a collection of marine plants. Get on with it.' Nobody had kept marine plants in captivity before, and most experts said it couldn't be done, which was very helpful. There was no literature, no expertise to refer to; I really was starting from scratch.

I sat down and thought about what I wanted, and I realized that what I really knew about was habitats, so I decided I'd base the collection around four different marine habitats. I had a little project room, and I set about trying to create the conditions of a mangrove swamp, a coral reef, a salt marsh and an intertidal rocky shore. I knew what I wanted to achieve, and it was just a process of trial and error before I could replicate the right conditions. At first I had just a couple of tanks: a trial rocky shore tank, with half a dozen seaweeds in it, and a trial salt-marsh tank, with some bits of sea lavender. Both of those are tidal habitats, so I pumped the water from one to the other to imitate the rise and fall of the tide. Eventually I found a way of doing all the things I needed to do, but it took a long time. In 1989 we were ready to start setting up the display tanks, and we opened in 1991 – that was six years after I'd first come to Kew!

I have quite a strange background, I suppose; I've done a lot of different things in my life before I landed here. My interest in marine things started at

PETER MORRIS
Manager of the
Marine and Aquatic
Displays

the age of two. I was born in Birmingham, and you can't get much further from the sea than that – but every time we went to stay in my grandmother's caravan at Muddiford, I'd be straight into the sea. I was under the water before I could even swim, and my poor father would turn blue standing around on the shore at Easter making sure I didn't get into trouble.

When I was 16 the family moved to Torquay – finally I was by the sea – and I joined the British Subaqua Club and learned to dive. The next year we moved to Worthing, by which time I'd left school. All I knew was that I wanted a job with animals – so I walked into the Brighton Aquarium and watched the dolphin show, and asked if there were any jobs going. There was a vacancy, as it happened – first of all in the aquarium, then later with the dolphins. I did pretty much every job imaginable at Brighton Aquarium, and I learned a lot.

TREE OF THE MONTH

Sweet chestnut *Castanea sativa*

LOCATION: Between the Stable Yard and the lake

DID YOU KNOW: This is probably the oldest tree in Kew, dating back at least to the early eighteenth century, possibly to the late seventeenth. There are several specimens in the area between the Stable Yard and the lake, probably the survivors of an old avenue leading to Richmond Lodge where George II lived. This particular one stands out because of the spiral growth habit of its trunk, a hangover from regular pollarding at earlier stages in its life.

Sweet chestnuts are among Kew's most successful trees – and are dependable providers of the gardens' spectacular show of autumn colour.

Then I met a guy who was importing coral-reef fish into an aquarium shop in Croydon, so I went to work for him for a while, and through him I met his Caribbean shipper. That gave me a chance to go on my first collecting trips, and I spent a year in Grenada learning the business from a different angle.

Sooner or later I had to come back to England because my passport was washed out in a shipwreck and they repatriated me. I ended up getting a job at a swimming pool in central London as a lifeguard, which I did for five years off and on. I didn't know what to do next, but a friend told me that I should contact the University of Bangor in North Wales, which is the leading marine biology college, and see what their attitude was towards mature students. Fortunately for me, the academic registrar was an algologist, a marine man, and very supportive of what I was trying to do, so he gave me an opportunity to get some A levels, which meant I could go on and do a joint honours degree in marine biology and botany.

I graduated from Bangor in 1982, but I couldn't find a job. I was getting quite despondent, but then quite by chance I picked up a copy of *New Scientist* and saw Kew's advert. I thought straight away that this was my job. I knew about aquaria, I knew about algae, I'd caught the fish…I was determined to get it.

Now I run all the marine and aquatic collection in Kew. That's in two places: the marine aquaria underneath the Palm House, and the six tropical tanks in the Princess of Wales Conservatory. I'm also responsible for the fish in the two major ponds. My job is a strange mixture, really, because I have to use so many different skills. I have to be a scientist and technician to maintain the habitats in the right state; I have to be a DIY fixer because if something goes wrong I need to mend it; and I need to know about the animals and plants, and make sure they're well and happy.

My day starts outside the Princess of Wales Conservatory, collecting leaves to give to the leafcutter ants for breakfast. They live in a tank underneath there, where they have their own fantastic fungus farm, and they're very popular with the visitors. In the spring and summer I try to give them Indian bean leaves; it's a nice broad leaf that's available right through into the autumn, and they eat every bit of it. If you give them other things they tend to eat a bit, then chuck the rest in the water and go boating on it – 20 or 30 of them sailing around the tank until they hit the tank wall and either capsize or climb up the glass wall and try to escape.

Once I've got the leaves, I go in and clean out the ant display. If I'm on my own I have to spray the poison-dart frog display with water to keep the habitat nice and moist, then I feed the fish in the top pond and the lily pond.

Then it's into the Palm House, where I have to clean the glass fronts, check the equipment, feed the fish and top up the tanks, because the water evaporates pretty quickly. If there's anything wrong, then I have to fix it. There are 250 separate pieces of equipment in the marine aquaria, any one of which could pack up at any time. A lot of the habitats are quite delicate, so you can't let things slide; if things go wrong, they must be fixed straight away. The European habitats have to be maintained at around 15°C (59°F), with an ambient air temperature of 25°C (77°F); if anything goes wrong with the cooling system we're in trouble. Three of the displays are tidal, so there's a lot of pumping equipment moving the water around, creating currents and circulation. We have filters to keep the water clean, lights to show the displays off, chillers to keep them cool…Things don't go wrong too often, but when they do it usually seems to be about six things at a time. I'm glad to say that casualties are very rare; I haven't bought a fish for the marine display for a couple of years now.

The freshwater stingray tank in the basement of the Princess of Wales Conservatory is a maintenance nightmare. Not only is there a lot of glass to clean – the tank comprises a series of viewing windows – but the fish themselves can cause problems for the unwary. Stingrays defend themselves with a series of sharp spines along the tail and each of these spines is equipped with stinging, thorn-like barbs that can deliver a painful jab to a potential attacker, so anyone who waded into the tank with bare feet – the water is only about 1.2 metres (4 feet) deep – would be in trouble. Even wearing boots wouldn't provide sufficient protection: stingrays have been known to penetrate heavy-duty rubber.

There is also the danger to the fish. Stingrays like nothing better than to bury themselves in the sand where, to the untrained eye, they are practically invisible.

Anyone wading in the tank could easily step on and crush one concealed in this way – and, as stingrays aren't particularly strong, this could be the end of it.

The tank does, however, need regular maintenance, to make sure rocks and filters are free of algae as well as to keep the windows clean. That's when I put my diving experience to good use. Every couple of weeks I change into my swimming trunks, don mask and snorkel, and go for a swim with the stingrays. There is enough water to dive in, so I float while I clean the inside of the tank. And if I do need to put a foot down on its sandy bottom, I'm sufficiently experienced to recognize the shadowy outline of a submerged stingray – which means nobody gets hurt, man or fish.

The real scientific focus of the marine collection is the algae. There are two types of algae: microalgae, which are tiny single-celled organisms that form the green or brown slime you have to scrape off a goldfish bowl, and macroalgae, which are basically seaweeds. They're simple plants; they take everything they need from the water they live in, so they don't need roots. As long as there's light and nitrogen, they're happy. It's impossible to overemphasize the importance of algae; they provide 50 per cent of the planet's oxygen, remove massive amounts of carbon dioxide and are the filters of the sea. If you didn't have them absorbing and recycling all the pollution you wouldn't be able to sustain any life in the sea at all. The plants utilize fish waste and turn it into food; the fish and the plants are totally dependent on each other.

ABOVE: One of Peter Morris' jobs is particularly unusual. In order to keep the viewing windows in the stingray tank clean and the rocks and filters free of algae, he has to swim inside the tank, taking care not to step on any of the fish.

But I was always aware that a few tanks full of seaweed wouldn't be very interesting to visitors, so what I've done is to create habitats where plants interact with animals. Plants in the land-based collection interact with animals all the time, particularly with insects and birds, so I thought it was important to create habitats here rather than just sterile displays. I've tried to introduce the right fauna for each habitat. In the rocky shore displays we've got various fish like wrasse and bass, and shellfish like limpets, mussels and winkles. In the mangroves we have the mudskippers – which, like the mangroves themselves, live both in and out of the water. They're true fish, with gills, but they're at home on land and in the water. I love the mudskippers; they're not very pretty, and there's a definite gender divide in people's reaction to them. Boys think they're great; girls tend to think they're horrible. We've also got archer fish in the mangroves. They're great animals – they catch their prey, which is mostly insects, by squirting water into the air and knocking things in. Sometimes they spit at us, especially at feeding time.

In the salt-marsh displays I've used mullet, which can thrive in varying degrees of salinity, and I put in a lot of fiddler crabs that I'd seen in Portugal. Originally this was going to be a British salt marsh, but the crabs are so great that I've changed my mind, and it's a European display.

The coral displays have the most colourful fish, of course, and we're also doing very well with soft corals. Occasionally we get sent a piece of hard coral by Customs and Excise if they've stopped someone from bringing it into the country. That's illegal, because removing it damages the reefs – but they can't just throw the coral away, and they can't ship it back, so they give it to us or to London Zoo.

With all those tanks to look after this can be a very demanding job. I can't take more than a week's holiday, and I have to be able to cover Christmas and other bank holidays if necessary. That's the downside of the job; you have to be completely devoted to the displays, and seeing as I live on site I sometimes get called out in the night as well. It has only happened twice, touch wood, but this is definitely a job that you can't forget about when you go home in the evening.

PUMPKIN FESTIVAL

The pumpkin festival takes place in and around the Waterlily House in October and has become one of the unmissable spectacles of Kew's year. Thousands of cucurbits – pumpkins, squashes and gourds – are displayed in a riot of colour, size and form; it's a great example of nature's extraordinary diversity, as well as a demonstration of the artistry of Kew's staff.

Preparation for the pumpkin festival starts in September, when the Waterlily House is cleaned out. Its usual residents are removed from the pond, where new waterlilies will be planted in the spring, and the water is drained. This is when the house gets its major annual clean up: everything is power-washed, from the glass

BELOW: For the annual pumpkin festival in October, over 3000 pumpkins, squashes and gourds are used to form a display celebrating the diversity of nature.

to the plumbing, in readiness for the autumn show. Phil Griffiths, manager of the glasshouses, then goes down to his supplier in Slindon, near Arundel in Sussex, to shop for cucurbits. With a budget of around £3500 he can buy an awful lot of them – more than enough to fill the 17-ton truck that brings his haul back to Kew. The fruits come in a bewildering variety, from the familiar orange pumpkin right through to extraordinary horned, striped gourds and strange bluish-grey squashes that look like alien life-forms. These are supplemented by home-grown varieties; there are pumpkin patches in the arboretum's nursery field, where Griffiths tries to raise some real monsters each year.

Visual impact is the key to a successful pumpkin festival, so it's important to find the right way to display this crazy collection. In 2003, rather than piling the fruits up on carts or bales of straw, as in previous years, Griffiths commissioned a special metal framework that would support them in a conical formation. Robin Brown of Brown Brothers in Watford came up with a kind of helter-skelter that would support the massive weight of 300-plus pumpkins of different shapes and sizes, without collapsing or letting parts of the display tumble into the pond. The result, designed and created by Emma Fox, was an extraordinary sight, reaching almost to the very top of the Waterlily House, with mounds of extra fruits tumbling in mad profusion around it. The cucurbits were hooked on to the framework without being damaged, and the display stayed absolutely intact for three weeks.

Keeping the fruits in good condition for the duration of the festival is important; anyone who's ever kept a Hallowe'en lantern for too long will know that a decaying pumpkin smells pretty rank. However, if they're undamaged they keep well enough to sell on to visitors after the display has been dismantled. Damaged fruits, of course, go straight to Kew's enormous mounds of compost and eventually provide food for the next year's plants. There's just one snag: cucurbit seeds are tough little things and don't always rot down, even in the biggest, hottest compost heaps. Big displays have resulted in a lot of weeds springing up in the gardens, wherever mulch has been laid. And an awful lot of those weeds have turned out to be pumpkins.

OPPOSITE: The sheer variety and number of pumpkins in the display make for a staggering spectacle in the Waterlily House.

NOVEMBER

Leaves are falling fast and it's time for the arboricultural team to get out and about, preparing the trees for a new year. You'll see trucks of steaming mulch being carted all over Kew, to be spread around the base of trees and on borders, putting back into the soil all the nutrients that a hard summer has taken out. November is a time for checking the old trees, felling or pruning anything in need of attention, and planting new trees that have been raised on site or brought in from outside. At Wakehurst Place the Christmas tree plantations are being harvested and, as the daylight fails, a thousand lights for the biggest of all the trees are being hoisted into place.

This month at Kew, don't miss
- The last of the autumn colour
- Strawberry trees west of King William's Temple and north of the Princess of Wales Conservatory
- The stunning Grass Garden

OPPOSITE: The tranquil Grass Garden, behind the Princess of Wales Conservatory, is at its best in November.

MANAGING THE HERBARIUM

Essentially an herbarium is a collection of dead plants. Everyone else at Kew laughs at us because they think we're only interested in things once they've died, but that's not true – not for all of us, at least. We now have a plot outside our Herbarium where people can grow things and get a bit of soil on their fingers, although I do actually believe that some of the old school really aren't much interested in plants until they've been collected and pressed.

I'm a botanist by training and background. My main job is managing the groups of regional botanists who work at Kew, and helping to manage the collection here in the Herbarium. We have teams working in countries around the world – Southeast Asia, drylands Africa, tropical America and so on. I have to make sure they have whatever they need for an expedition in terms of money and equipment, I have to apply for funding if it's needed, and I have to oversee

DANIELA ZAPPI
Assistant Keeper for
the Regional Teams
at the Herbarium

the management of the collection once it's brought back here to Kew. Sometimes I go out with them – I've been to Cameroon recently, and I try to visit Brazil when I can, because that's where I'm from so it's very close to my heart. But the teams have to be based at Kew because that's a good way of maintaining the quality of the collections and making sure our Herbarium is up to standard.

An expedition will usually visit conservation sites that the government of the country is prepared to protect. They provide the government with information in the form of a baseline list of species found, then they break that down into what's endemic to the region, what's more important, what's threatened and so on. It's an overall survey of an area, finding out what's growing where, adding to our global picture but also providing governments with the knowledge they need to conserve their native flora.

A field trip hasn't changed much since the nineteenth century, really; you're still cutting specimens, drying them, pressing them and annotating them. You'll make a blanket collection of all the species in an area, then you bring them back to the university or the hotel and you press them straight away. The equipment has changed a little, but not a lot. Nowadays we have a special drying rack like a set of shelves, which we set up over a gas stove. The specimens are placed between two sheets of newspaper and left to dry for around 48 hours, then bagged up and dispatched. On a good day you might get up to 200 samples — and they all have to be labelled, either by hand or by computer.

When the teams aren't out in the field they're back here identifying and classifying their material, and there's a huge demand on the resources of the Herbarium in that respect. Some of the material they bring in will stay here to add to our collection; if there are duplicates, we'll log them and identify them and then maybe pass them on to other herbaria around the world. Everyone wants their stuff to be identified by a place like Kew — there aren't many herbaria that offer this service, and people know that we have a huge amount of knowledge about certain areas.

Packages come into the Herbarium from all over the world; not just from our own teams, but from botanists in many countries who need us to identify a specimen. They might know the genus but not the species, and the only way they can establish that firmly is by having it identified by us; smaller herbaria just don't have the bibliography or the staff time. A Kew identification upgrades the value of a collection, and it helps us to gather information about what other people have, so it works both ways.

Plant specimens arrive packaged up in our post room, and they're immediately opened, placed into a plastic bag to retain their humidity, and put straight into the deep freeze at -20°C (-4°F) for three to five days. That kills off any possible pests or diseases, and because they keep their moisture they don't get too brittle. The collections management unit is a crazy place; we send things all over the world as well, either as loans or gifts, and there are packages flooding in all the time. It's like Christmas Day down there sometimes.

The Herbarium contains some items that were collected in the eighteenth century, and quite a large amount from the nineteenth century, when various different collections were amalgamated and brought here. We have the Amazonian collection of Richard Spruce, a botanist who worked in Peru, Ecuador and Brazil in the 1850s, which is full of species that were brand new to science at that time. We have his collecting books here, which are very important; you can see his

PLANT OF THE MONTH

Miscanthus sinensis

WHERE TO SEE IT: Grass Garden

DID YOU KNOW: *Miscanthus sinensis* is one of the most commonly grown ornamental grasses in Britain; it's fast catching up with pampas grass, even though it was only introduced to the horticultural trade in western Europe in the 1970s. A Chinese native, it boasts huge dangling seed heads in the late autumn, but its attractions don't end there: it's currently being researched in Kew's Jodrell Laboratory as an alternative renewable fuel and fibre source for rural populations.

Miscanthus sinensis is just one of 550 species growing in the Grass Garden, and many of them are at their best in November when the seed heads are at their fullest. The garden is certainly one of the most rewarding places to visit when the rest of Kew is putting itself to bed for the winter, especially as frost or low winter sun can illuminate the variety of different seed heads in spectacular ways.

incredibly neat handwriting from the field, where he would have been hot, wet and bothered by mosquitoes. We know from his diaries that he was frequently ill, and that the conditions would have been very insanitary, but still he wrote these neat, precise remarks, full of exclamation marks, right out there in some little shack in the field.

We have a bit of Charles Darwin's material from his trip on the *Beagle* – about 20 or 30 sheets, which we're very proud to show to visitors. It's not the age of these items that's so important as the wealth of new species that they show; from about 1810 onwards you can see all these fantastic botanists succeeding each other, discovering new things that have now become rare or endangered.

Kew's Herbarium contains a priceless collection, and we have to strike a balance between protecting and preserving those historical documents, and making them accessible to people who need them. One of our major projects at the moment is creating a database, so that people can access the collection without necessarily having to handle the specimens. The older ones are getting very fragile, and so the less handling they receive the better. We've developed a way of creating digital images of the specimens, which can be emailed to botanists anywhere in the world. We've built a special scanner, which scans the sheets from above so that you don't have to lay them face down or squash them with a hood. Digital images will never lose their purity, and they're so easy to store and handle. Over the next five years we hope to get a substantial amount of the collection digitized – we've only scratched the surface so far, and we have to start doing it in a systematic way. The only trouble is that by showing people what we've got here, the demands on the collection are actually increasing; more and more people want to come to Kew to see the Herbarium for themselves.

Four days of my week are spent as a manager; I try to keep Fridays clear to do some actual botany. My current area of interest is the coffee family, Rubiaceae, so every Friday I write 'Mrs Rubiaceae' in my diary and I won't make any other appointments if I can help it.

I came to England in 1991; before that I'd been studying botany at the University of São Paulo in Brazil, with no plans to leave the country at all. It

came about because of a cactus. I was doing a masters degree on cacti, and while I was out in the field I came across a species that I had never seen before – a real beauty with blue flowers and blue fruits. I didn't know what it was, and the pressed specimen spent some months with me until I could identify it. When I got back to the university I looked through all the books, but I still couldn't find it – and then I got in touch with Nigel Taylor, a cactus specialist from Kew who was on a field trip in Brazil at the time. He was visiting the university, and I was assigned as his minder; well, I must have looked after him very well, because I ended up marrying him.

It turned out that the cactus I'd discovered was a new species, which we named *Cipocereus laniflorus*. Both the cactus and I were transplanted to Kew, where we're now flourishing.

When Nigel and I got together we looked carefully at my job in Brazil, and his job in Kew, and we decided that things would be better for us if I came to England. He had good prospects here, whereas I was just about to start a PhD, so I came over in 1991 and started working at Kew in 1992, when a job came up databasing species. Then I transferred into the main Herbarium on the condition that I wouldn't study cacti, as Nigel was already doing that – hence my project on Rubiaceae. Now Nigel's moved on to another job, so I'm doing cacti as well.

Moving to England was a very steep learning curve for me. I didn't speak much English, so that was my priority because not only did I have to get a job, I had to finish my PhD and then translate it into English for publication. I did all that in less than a year, and then got a job! There were times at first when I felt very isolated, because the cultures are so different, and whenever a colleague

came to visit from Brazil I glued myself to that person and spent all the time talking Portuguese.

ABOVE: Over 7 million specimens of dried material are housed in Kew's Herbarium, including a few sheets sourced by Charles Darwin.

I try to go back to Brazil every year if I can. Nigel and I have two daughters now, eight and six years old, so we can't uproot ourselves that easily – but we're bringing the girls up to be completely bilingual, and I want them to grow up aware of their mother's culture. Nigel speaks perfect Portuguese now – he can even lecture in it at the university in São Paulo – and that's what we tend to speak at home. We take a long break in summer and we all go to Brazil. The girls stay with their grandmother, and Nigel and I go out into the field. It's a holiday for the children, but it tends to be work for us. I like to keep close contacts with fieldwork in Brazil, because that will always be where my professional heart is. At the moment I'm more a manager than a botanist, but the position rotates every three years so soon I'll be going back to what I trained for. It's important that botanists should have management experience, because it makes you more efficient at managing your own research projects – but I certainly wouldn't want to do it for the rest of my life. I'm not the corporate type. I always want to get back to Mrs Rubiaceae at the end of the week.

FALLEN LEAVES

Once upon a time, autumn at Kew was one long back-breaking round of raking dead leaves and carting them away. But attitudes and technology have changed, and the leaves are now dealt with very differently. In the more formal parts of the garden, the staff use blowers instead of rakes, so clearing these areas of Kew is a much easier task than it used to be.

In the arboretum itself the leaves are dealt with *in situ* – unlike all other waste at Kew they aren't added to the compost heaps in the Stable Yard. They are poor in nutrients by the time they fall in autumn as the trees have reabsorbed everything they need to store up for the next growing season, and this means that while dead leaves are good for breaking up soil, they're not much use for feeding. So the grass-cutting team doesn't remove them; instead it shreds them, using specially adapted mulching decks on the back of rotary mowers. A single leaf goes through the mulcher and comes out in about 50 pieces. This organic litter is left around the base of the trees, where it can easily be taken down into the soil by earthworms, who are unable to tackle a whole leaf until it has rotted down. So the trees get their soil conditioned, the worms get food and the Kew staff have their workload lightened – it's good news all round.

OPPOSITE: The fallen autumn leaves provide a visual treat for visitors, but they also create a lot of work for the staff at Kew.

THE FRANCIS ROSE RESERVE

Lichens, mosses and liverworts aren't the most sensational plants and fungi in Kew's collection – yet, in terms of biodiversity in the United Kingdom, this group, known as cryptogams, are probably the country's most important. 'Flowering plants grab our attention,' says Andy Jackson, head of Wakehurst Place in Sussex, 'but it's the shy and retiring mosses, liverworts and lichens that are Britain's most significant contribution to biodiversity. The rest of Europe is much richer than we are in flowering plants, but because we have such a profoundly oceanic climate we have an amazingly rich variety of mosses.'

These humble stars of the Royal Botanic Gardens at Wakehurst Place have been recognized at last with the creation of the Francis Rose Reserve – 25 hectares (62 acres) of deeply incised valley that boast a bewildering diversity of mosses, lichens and liverworts. The reserve is named in honour of the man who did more than anyone else to draw attention to the importance of these plants: Francis Rose MBE was one of the first botanists to identify this group as an important indicator of environmental health. 'Francis is an amazing man who, in my estimation, will never be emulated in terms of his contribution to our understanding of biodiversity in the UK,' says Andy Jackson. 'His knowledge is amazing, of course: he can identify thousands of different species just by looking at them. But he was one of the first people to bring an ecological perspective to his work.'

In the 1970s Francis Rose became one of the first botanists to use lichens to draw attention to the dangers of pollution. He discovered he could create a 'weather map' of the United Kingdom that showed the areas affected by sulphur dioxide, based on the presence or absence of lichens. An industrial pollutant, the gas is the main cause of acid rain. Today people are aware of the impact that pollution has on pristine areas – that acid rain falls on the highlands of Scotland, for instance, even though the sulphur dioxide that is responsible comes from the north of England.

Francis Rose's connection with the Sussex Weald goes back to 1948, when he started visiting its characteristic sandstone outcrops – a favourite habitat for the mosses, liverworts and lichens that were his lifelong interest. Getting around the area wasn't easy in the 1940s, when much of the Weald was still owned by private landowners and there were far fewer roads, so Rose was obliged to do

most of his fieldwork on a bicycle. But his doggedness paid off; he alerted landowners to the importance of the habitats in their possession, and English Nature to the value of these endangered areas. The result was that whole parts of Kent and Sussex were nominated as sites of Special Scientific Interest, thus preserving them from the ravages of developers in the post-war years.

In 2001 Andy Jackson suggested to Peter Crane, director of the Royal Botanic Gardens, Kew, that they should honour Francis Rose with the creation of the reserve at Wakehurst that now bears his name. 'It was a way of highlighting this group of plants, really. When you have a group of organisms that don't have a lot of charisma, one of the best ways to bring them to the attention of the public is through a charismatic human being – and that's Francis.'

The decision to protect mosses, liverworts and lichens caused instant conflict. Wakehurst Place is famous in the UK for its rhododendrons – and rhododendrons

ABOVE: The Francis Rose Reserve at Wakehurst Place is home to a huge variety of mosses, lichens and liverworts, which thrive on the sandstone outcrops.

are Public Enemy Number One when it comes to mosses and liverworts. *Rhododendron ponticum* is the greatest possible threat to the sandstone sites it invades, as it leaves a massive seed deposit that germinates and then shades out everything else, creating a monoculture. A single seedling can grow to 1.2 metres (4 feet) within three years, and when pulled out it sprouts again almost immediately. It is as invasive, and as much of a threat, as Japanese knotweed.

Andy Jackson, with the support of Francis Rose, advocated the removal of thousands of rhododendrons and the smaller plants now flourish on the Wakehurst site, where outcrops of Ardingly sandstone make a perfect habitat for some of the rarest species. It's a very special stone, so porous that it will always wick water to its surface, allowing moisture-loving plants to cling to life in areas where there isn't usually enough rain. The reserve is currently home to about 220 different species of lichen, 35 liverworts and 50 mosses – and there are more to come.

Francis Rose recorded the slender threadmoss (*Orthodontium gracile*) at Wakehurst in 1991. The plant, which is only known from seven sites in Britain, hasn't been recorded there since, but the plan is to reintroduce it to the reserve by cultivating spores on pieces of sandstone and then gluing the pieces back into the wild. Thanks to new techniques of micropropagation, new plants can be brought on from spores that have been stored in liquid nitrogen, and the success rate is pretty high. Moss is generally regarded as a nuisance – something that ruins lawns and blocks gutters – but it's an incredibly important plant group in the UK and this will be the first example of reintroducing a moss from culture in Britain.

Climate change is a challenge to the Francis Rose Reserve, which may be too dry to sustain certain plants, like the filmy fern that flourished on the Weald in damper times. Botanists at Wakehurst are doing everything they can to restore the fern population; and educating visitors about this and other aspects of their work is hugely important. A total of two-thirds of the reserve is divided into three visitable areas. The first one, called 'Wow!', provides views of the rocks and enables visitors to appreciate the real richness of the plant life. The second area, 'Ouch!', shows how these habitats can be trashed by human activity. It has been a picnic site since 1965 and unfortunately the plant population has been destroyed by children sliding on the rocks, people carving graffiti and so on. 'How Can You Help?', the third area, is full of information about how biodiversity can be protected in private gardens. These cover one per cent of Britain – a huge amount of habitat. The main message there is that alien invasive plants are the single greatest threat to British wildlife, and visitors are encouraged to think about what they buy – and to be careful about how they dispose of garden waste. Japanese knotweed has spread through the UK because of fly-tipping in fields, and many habitats have been destroyed simply because people don't think before they dump plant waste.

TREE OF THE MONTH

Maidenhair tree *Ginkgo biloba*

LOCATION: Near the Secluded Garden

DID YOU KNOW: In 2002 this male *Ginkgo biloba* was named one of 50 'Great British Trees' in honour of the Queen's Golden Jubilee. It certainly is one of the star players at Kew, where it has lived since its original planting in 1762 (which makes it one of the 'old lions').

Ginkgos come originally from Asia, and were introduced into Europe in the 1750s. Eighteenth-century arboriculturists at Kew weren't sure just how hardy the tree would be, so they planted it against the wall of the great stove house for a bit of protection. The building was demolished in 1861, but by that time the ginkgo was well established, and has continued to thrive in the same spot ever since. Now it's one of Kew's autumn highlights: its leaves turn a wonderful bright yellow in November.

DECEMBER

The trees are bare again, the fallen leaves have gone, and the only colour comes from the unexpected flash of a bright red stem or the pinks and purples of berries. Jasmines and cherries do their best as well, but December is a time to enjoy the bare skeleton of Kew, the sun low in the sky, the naked trees casting long shadows across the scant lawns. In the shop, shoppers and revellers are gathering in celebration of Christmas, while on the lakes there are even greater crowds of moorhens, coots, mallard, tufted duck and pochard, who have cruised into Kew to find a safe place to spend the hardest part of winter.

This month at Kew, don't miss
- Christmas Festivals at Kew and Wakehurst Place
- Holly Walk
- Berry and bark colour throughout the gardens
- The winter-flowering cherry trees
- The Winter Garden, Wakehurst Place

OPPOSITE: December is the perfect month to enjoy both the fine architectural lines of Kew's glasshouses and the warmth they provide on a frosty day.

THE CHRISTMAS FESTIVAL

Kew is as magical in December as it is at any other time of the year. On a sunny winter's day the bare branches of trees are at their best in pale winter sunshine, and frost outlines structures and shapes that are hidden during other months. There's a surprising amount of colour to be seen, too, from the familiar red berries of holly through to the less expected floral delights of viburnums, hellebores and witch hazels.

And for the run-up to Christmas Kew focuses its efforts on a programme of special seasonal events that keep the turnstiles turning through what was once the quietest time of the year. Father Christmas pays a visit to Kew, usually to a wooded dell in White Peaks, where he receives throngs of enthusiastic young visitors. There's live music throughout the gardens at weekends: a brass quintet at Victoria Gate or a vocal quartet in the Orangery. And there's a great deal of activity around the shops, where a growing range of toys, food and plants is on offer.

Kew Gardens normally shuts at quarter past four during the winter, but before Christmas the hours are extended until eight every Friday and Saturday evening. And as darkness falls the gardens are transformed. Some trees are decorated with thousands of lights, others are uplit in different colours, and dozens of Christmas trees are placed around the pond. The glasshouses look good too: the Palm House, although not open in the evenings, is lit from outside and the Princess of Wales Conservatory from within. The latter provides a warm refuge on a cold winter evening. Around the Main Gate, the coming of Christmas is marked with extravagant displays of wreaths and bows.

Wakehurst Place also does Christmas in style. It has the country's tallest-growing Christmas tree, illuminated with a thousand lights, and there are home-grown Christmas trees for sale. Their major carol service is very popular as well.

The Christmas Festival is one of Kew's biggest annual activities. Not only does it provide a place to shop and celebrate; it also focuses attention on the unsung beauties of the gardens in winter. And these are closed on only two days: Christmas Eve and Christmas Day. Staff who live on site celebrate at home, security guards keep an eye on things and there is some basic plant care to be done – but for those two days in the year, Kew is quiet.

OPPOSITE: The gardens are often filled with fairy lights and music, making Christmas at Kew a very special time of year.

STUDYING PLANT PROPERTIES

My main interest is plant chemistry – the naturally produced compounds in plants that have a whole range of functions and uses. They're often called 'secondary metabolytes', because they're not absolutely essential to the plant's survival in the way that, say, chlorophyll is. But in many ways they're just as important. Pigment is a good example; it creates colourful flowers that attract insects and thus allows the plant to reproduce. A lot of plants wouldn't be pollinated if they couldn't attract insects, so those pigments play a vital role.

The compounds I'm particularly interested in are those that mediate or effect biological interaction. There are a lot of chemicals, for instance, that protect a plant against predators; that's a perfect example of biological interaction. Plants can't move, they can't run away – so they have to develop different defence mechanisms. Some of them have spines or leathery leaves, some are too tough to chew, others produce silica in their leaves, which insects can't get through. But the more interesting ones from my point of view are the plants that produce chemicals to protect themselves against predators or bacteria or fungi.

Once you've identified some kind of biological activity in these plants, you can start to study all sorts of possible uses for that compound. On a basic level, plant chemistry gives us a greater understanding of how natural systems work; there might be a poison, for instance, that puts off insects or kills fungus spores. But if you take it further than that, you might find that a particular chemical compound could have a lot of other applications. The plant kingdom is a huge, amazing pharmacopoeia, and there are thousands of new medicines out there waiting to be discovered. Plant chemistry is actually quite a small field, and not very well funded, but when you consider that many of the world's best-selling medicines are of plant or fungal origin, you can see how important it is.

I'm particularly interested in British plants with traditional medical properties, and I'm trying to find out what the basis for those traditions are. Take figwort, or *Scrophularia*, a relative of the snapdragon. The old texts describe it as a wound-healer – but why? We did a collaborative project with King's College, London, to find out if there was any truth in the tradition, and it turned out that certain compounds derived from *Scrophularia* actually stimulate the growth of fibroblasts,

PHIL
STEVENSON
Plant Chemist

the cells in connective tissue that grow round a wound. So the old use ascribed to figwort was real – it does help a wound to heal if you put it around a cut.

My main project at the moment is looking at how crops protect themselves against insects and diseases. If we can find out how nature does it, then we can encourage farmers to be less dependent on pesticides. Our particular focus is on farmers in developing countries, where there are huge pest problems and where emerging economies can't afford to lose their crops.

My pet crop is chickpeas. Most of us in Europe know the chickpea as an ingredient in hummus and falafel; some of us have eaten chana masala in Indian restaurants. But chickpeas are a really important staple crop: they're used to make gram flour for bread and biscuits, and for many farmers all over Southeast Asia they're a major livelihood pulse. Chickpeas are vulnerable to wilt, a form of fungal attack that causes the growing tops to rot off – but the wild relatives of the chickpea, which grow in the mountains of central Asia, have an inbuilt defence against that particular fungus.

I went over to India and looked at a lot of those wild relatives, and discovered that there are several chemical compounds in them that you don't find in the cultivated varieties. Some of those compounds, it turns out, are very active against fungus. They're clever plants, the legumes: they tend to produce those chemicals only when they need them, so they're not wasting energy. If they're attacked by fungi, they'll produce tiny amounts of the chemicals at the point of infection. A fungal spore germinates in the soil near a root, for instance, and the cells that are near the spore will start to produce defensive chemicals. That activity has been bred out of some commercial varieties, so we now have to breed it back in.

Once we've identified a useful chemical like that, we have to get it back into the plants. We do this through breeding programmes, transferring pollen from one plant to another to create hybrids. The hybrids are created by good old-fashioned breeding methods. Once we've created a strain that is biologically active, we encourage the farmers to start using that seed – and once they've got it, that's it, the plants will fertilize each other and there's no more need for fungicides.

Insects are the other big problem for farmers in India. The pod–borer moth is one of the worst insects in the world. Its caterpillar destroys cotton, pulses, tomatoes, in fact just about anything it can get its teeth into. Farmers tend to spray against it at the moment, but we've discovered various chemical compounds in pulse crops that mediate some kind of interaction with the pod–borer. There are some chemicals in the leaves that actually seem to stimulate the female to lay her eggs there, so we're interested in getting rid of them! It's a reverse approach to the way we're tackling wilt; we're trying to breed something out, rather than in.

Anything we can do to bring down the use of pesticides is a good thing. It's not just because they're generally bad for the environment, although of course they are. There are huge toxicity problems for the farmers, who never wear the right protective gear when they're spraying. And the insects are developing resistance to the insecticide. We hear a lot of horror stories, which sadly are so common now that they don't make the news any more, about farmers whose crops have failed because the insecticides didn't work, and who go bankrupt with no hope of paying off their debts. And all too often they end up using the insecticide to commit suicide. It couldn't kill the moths, but it kills human beings very effectively.

Some of my work is done in the field, collecting specimens and finding out how plants behave in the wild, but when it comes to analyzing the chemical composition of a plant, that's done back at the Jodrell Laboratory here at Kew. We grow specimens in the nurseries, then we run a 'bioassay' on them in the lab. That means we make a sort of herbal tea using various solvents like alcohol, then we isolate the various chemicals in there using a whole range of machinery – mass spectrometers, nuclear-magnetic resonance spectrometers, UV spectrometers and so on. In chickpeas we've actually identified six or seven totally new chemicals, compounds that are new to science, and that's a real lifter. It's a bit like a botanist discovering a new species of plant. Those compounds are so rich with potential, you might be stumbling across something with a major ecological or medicinal use.

Another area of work that we do in the Jodrell Laboratory is authentication – analyzing specimens that are sent to us to find out what they really are. There's a lot of interest at the moment in alternative medicine, so we get practitioners sending us herbal remedies to check that they really are what they say they are. Traditional Chinese remedies, for instance, are often mixtures of different dried plant material, and you have to be very certain of what they are before you start using them. Once the seed, bark or root is dried and ground up, it's absolutely impossible to recognize it, and that can be dangerous. There was a notorious case in Belgium not so long ago when there was a batch of Chinese herbal medicine going round that contained *Aristolochia*, a type of climbing plant that's very poisonous and can cause kidney failure and even death. It looks very similar to another plant that's commonly used in remedies, and it had been gathered by mistake. Fourteen Belgian ladies died because they'd been taking a supposed slimming compound that contained *Aristolochia*.

I've been working at the Jodrell on and off since I was a student, and I can't imagine working anywhere else now. I have a split appointment with the

OVERLEAF: *After the recent restoration of its exterior, Kew Palace, set off by a light fall of snow, appears once again as a residence fit for a king.*

University of Greenwich, with whom Kew does some joint projects, and so I have the best of both worlds. Kew has such status in the world of plant chemistry, and the Jodrell Laboratory has the best equipment you could wish for. Sometimes I find myself thinking about whether I should be moving on, but where would I go? I've got everything I need here to do the work I really want to do – and in my lunch hour I can nip out the door and go and see the crocus carpet or the autumn leaves. Not many scientists can do that.

TREE OF THE MONTH

Giant redwood *Sequoiadendron giganteum*

LOCATION: Wakehurst Place

DID YOU KNOW: The 30-metre (100-foot) Californian giant redwood or wellingtonia is decorated every December to become one of the biggest Christmas trees in the country. A thousand light bulbs are strung around it, supported on a web of ropes that will take their weight if there are high winds. A 64-metre (210-foot) crane hoists the lights up above the tree and spirals them down on to the ropes and branches, like icing being piped on to a cake.

When the Wakehurst Christmas tree is fully lit, from the beginning of December through to Twelfth Night, it can be seen from high points up to 22 kilometres (14 miles) away – and sightings have been reported by pilots flying out of Paris's Charles de Gaulle airport. It forms the centrepiece for Wakehurst's Christmas festivities, when 2000 local people sing carols in the open air of the carriage ring outside the house.

Wakehurst Place leads the field in introducing alternative types of Christmas tree to the British public, through a programme of commercial forestry that produces over 1000 trees every year. The traditional Norway spruce remains popular, accounting for about 40 per cent of sales – but if not properly cared for, its spiky needles drop easily, making the January clean-up a nightmare. Other trees, like the silver firs, have softer needles that stay on longer. There are even giant redwoods for big living rooms – Wakehurst sells some fine specimens about 4.5 metres (15 feet) tall.

After Christmas, trees can be brought to Wakehurst where they will be chipped – for free. And the chips are taken away to be used as mulch in the garden.

SCIENTIFIC RESEARCH

Tucked away at the north end of the Order Beds, the Jodrell Laboratory isn't the most interesting-looking building in Kew – but it's home to some of the most exciting work being carried out at the Royal Botanic Gardens. For many years, Jodrell scientists have been examining the chemical compounds in plants, building up profiles of each species and identifying those that have some kind of biological activity. With massive advances in this kind of chemical profiling and the harnessing of DNA analysis to provide further data about the relationship among plants, Kew is able to apply its research work to some surprising fields of inquiry.

A CURE FOR CANCER?

Once the chemical profile for a plant compound shows some kind of biological activity it can be compared with other active compounds to find out where it might be useful. Naturally, one of the first areas of inquiry was potential anticancer activity – and it soon emerged that certain plants have very similar profiles to known anticancer drugs. In fact, many cancer drugs used today are derived from plants.

Certain global health trends influenced the direction the work took at this stage. In some parts of China and Japan, for instance, there has been a marked rise in stomach and bowel cancer in recent years – these are common diseases in the West, but ones that had, until then, been comparatively rare in the East. Working on the hypothesis that there may be a dietary cause for this, scientists in the Jodrell Laboratory noticed a shift in eating habits among people in the affected areas, who were switching increasingly from wild forms of rice to new cultivated varieties. So they compared the chemical profiles of cultivated rice with its wild relatives, and found that several chemical compounds were lost during the commercial processing of the grain. These compounds have cancer-protective activity.

It's possible, therefore, that commercial milling of rice is robbing this staple food of its beneficial anticancer chemicals, leaving hitherto healthy populations at risk of developing the disease. The next stage for the Jodrell scientists, in partnership with the World Cancer Fund and Leicester University, is to test this hypothesis and find out whether the chemical compounds in wild rice really do have anticancer properties.

STOPPING THE SPREAD OF HIV

Work on insects in the Jodrell Laboratory suggested that certain chemical compounds prevent the effective digestion of food. Insects dosed with them could eat and eat, but would still starve to death. The compounds stop the normal absorption of food – and this means they could do all sorts of other things as well. These compounds inhibit enzymes that are involved in cell-to-cell recognition. And this, it appears, may stop the spread of viruses.

A virus spreads in an infected body by moving from cell to cell. An infected cell comes into contact with the membrane of a healthy cell, they adhere and the virus hops across. The same thing happens with cancer: cells meet, adhere and

PLANT OF THE MONTH

Viburnum *Viburnum × bodnantense* 'Dawn'

WHERE TO SEE IT: Museum Border near Victoria Gate; Woodland Garden; Wakehurst Place

DID YOU KNOW: At a time when much of Kew Gardens is bare, the winter-flowering viburnums are putting on one of the best shows to be seen at any time of the year. The 'Dawn' cultivar is particularly rewarding, with bunches of pink flowers on the end of bare twigs – and they smell good too!

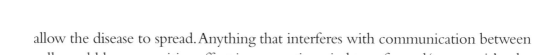

allow the disease to spread. Anything that interferes with communication between cells could have a positive effect in preventing viral transfer and 'metastasis' – the process of rapid cell-multiplication involved in cancer.

CRACKING DOWN ON DRUGS

Chemical profiling isn't the only tool at the disposal of Kew's scientists. They are also analyzing plant DNA. Just as human DNA can differentiate between individuals, so the DNA of a plant can provide reliable data about where it grew – samples can differ widely in plants of the same species that were gathered in different locations. There is potential here for developing a useful tool for the war against the drugs trade, as Customs and Excise could use plant DNA profiles to pinpoint the sources of illegal drugs like cocaine, cannabis and heroin.

MEDICINE FOR MALARIA

Traditional cures for malaria in areas of Brazil and Africa often use plant substances, but until recently there has been little attempt to understand how and why these ancient remedies work. Jodrell scientists are working in partnership with local groups to study traditional malaria medicine, investigating the chemistry and molecular biology of the plants used in the treatment of the disease.

Ritual and tradition govern the preparation of these 'fever medicines', and it seems that there are sound scientific reasons for practices that were once thought to be of religious significance only. Tradition dictates, for instance, that the plants are collected only from certain sacred spots – and chemical profiling shows that plants from these locations have a different molecular fingerprint from specimens grown in other places. The preparation of the medicines is often complex, governed by ceremonies that involve singing and chanting – which could be a traditional way of preparing the plant material for the right amount of time. And scientists have observed that the same rituals are performed in many separate communities. One example is discarding the water in which the plant was first boiled. It was thought that this was based on vague notions of purification – but it now appears that the water from the first boiling contains undesirable toxins,

while that from the second boiling retains beneficial compounds and is not dangerous to the patient.

An Amazonian plant, abuta, contains alkaloid compounds that could be of major use in the global treatment of malaria, and these will be undergoing further trials in Brazil in the next few years. Old wives' tales and plant-related superstitions, it seems, often contain scientific truths far more subtle than has previously been suspected. And, with the breakdown of village life in many African countries, and the disappearance of traditional medicine men, it's more important than ever to harvest this knowledge before it's lost for good — particularly as the incidence of malaria is increasing.

ABOVE: The Queen's Garden contains plants that were used medicinally in the seventeenth century. Today, scientists at Kew study plants in an attempt to find cures for many modern diseases.

Index

This book is published to accompany the television series entitled *A Year at Kew*, first broadcast on BBC2 in 2004.

Executive producer: Jeremy Gibson
Series producer: Adam Alexander
Producer/Director: Tim Green

Published by BBC Books,
BBC Worldwide Limited,
Woodlands, 80 Wood Lane,
London W12 0TT

First published 2004
Text © BBC Worldwide Ltd and the Trustees of the Royal Botanic Gardens, Kew 2004
The moral right of the author has been asserted.

ISBN 0 563 52108 2

Set in Bembo
Printed and bound in Italy by LEGO SpA
Colour separations by Radstock Reproductions Ltd, Midsomer Norton

Commissioning editor: Nicky Ross
Project editor: Sarah Miles
Copy editor: Tessa Clark
Designer: Isobel Gillan
Production controller: Arlene Alexander
Jacket art direction: Pene Parker

BBC Books would like to thank the following Kew staff for their invaluable help:
Fiona Bradley, Dom Costello, Gina Fullerlove, Catherine Gilhooly, Stewart Henchie, Andy Jackson, Tony Kirkham, John Lonsdale, Lucinda Matthews, Andrew McRobb, James Morley, Hannah Rogers, Monique Simmonds, Nigel Taylor.

For more information on the Royal Botanic Gardens, Kew see www.kew.org or telephone 020 8332 5655. To join the Friends of Kew or to make a gift to support Kew's important work, telephone 020 8332 5922.

BBC Worldwide would like to thank the following for providing photographs and for permission to reproduce copyright material. While every effort has been made to trace and acknowledge copyright holders, we would like to apologize should there be any errors or omissions.

BBC (Laurence Cendrowicz) 55, 81, 95, 107, 121; Jonathan Buckley 61; Garden Picture Library/Howard Rice 144; Harpur Garden Library 133; Tony Kirkham 127; Marianne Majerus 106; Clive Nichols Garden Pictures 91; Derek St Romaine Photography 123, 150; The Trustees of the Royal Botanic Gardens, Kew 11, 20, (Tudor Harwood) 142, 169, (Roger Howard) 2, (Paul Little) 21, 34, 38, 41, 183, (Milan Svanderlik) 57, (Ron Zabeau) 17.

All other photographs by Andrew McRobb © The Trustees of the Royal Botanic Gardens, Kew.

Page 2: An aerial view of the Temperate House at Kew